Map from Classroom Atlas
© 1994 by Rand McNally, R.L. 94-S-72

Enchantment of the World

LUXEMBOURG

By Emilie U. Lepthien

Consultants for Luxembourg: Alexander B. Murphy, Ph.D., Department of Geography, University of Oregon, Eugene, Oregon, and Dr. Jul Christophory, Director, Bibliothèque Nationale, Luxembourg

Consultant for Reading: Robert L. Hillerich, Ph.D., Bowling Green State University, Bowling Green, Ohio

CHILDRENS PRESS®
CHICAGO

Even in well-populated areas, small gardens are nurtured.

For Vivian Norris, lifelong friend

Library of Congress Cataloging-in-Publication Data

Lepthien, Emilie U. (Emilie Utteg)
  Luxembourg / by Emilie U. Lepthien.
    p.   cm. — (Enchantment of the world)
  Includes index.
  Summary: An introduction to the geography, history, government, economy, culture, and people of one of the smallest and oldest independent countries in Europe.
  ISBN 0-516-02714-X
  1. Luxembourg—Juvenile literature.
[1. Luxembourg.] I. Title. II. Series.
DH905.L47 1989   89-34664
949.35—dc20   CIP
                                               AC

Picture Acknowledgments
AP/Wide World Photos, Inc.: 28 (2 photos), 29, 107
Arbed Corporation: 44
The Bettmann Archive: 17, 24 (bottom), 27
© **Cameramann International Ltd.:** 10 (right), 14 (bottom), 18, 39 (left), 48 (right), 59, 76, 82 (bottom left), 91, 95, 111 (left)

© **Emilie Lepthien:** 4, 14 (top), 33 (2 photos), 34, 65, 68, 71 (left), 74, 86 (top right), 87, 89 (right), 93 (top right), 103 (2 photos), 112
The Marilyn Gartman Agency: © Ellis Herwig, 52, 64
The Granger Collection, New York: 14 (center), 20 (left), 21 (left), 23
H. Armstrong Roberts: 12
Historical Pictures Service, Chicago: 21 (right), 24 (top), 39 (right)
North Wind Picture Archives: 20 (right)
© **Chip & Rosa Maria Peterson:** 9 (right), 10 (left), 60 (right), 61, 67, 69, 110 (bottom left & bottom right)
Photri: 8, 9 (left), 11 (right), 41, 47, 51, 54, 60 (left), 62, 70, 71 (right), 80, 82 (top), 86 (left), 93 (left), 94 (2 bottom photos), 97 (left), 99 (2 photos), 100, 110 (top), 111 (right), 120, 121
Root Resources: © **Rodeghier**, 5, 81, 89 (left), 94 (top), 97 (right); © **Jane Kriete**, 36, 82 (bottom right), 96; © **Russel A. Kriete**, 75, 93 (bottom right), 98
TSW-Click/Chicago, Ltd.: © **Dallas & John Heaton**, 6, 88
Shostal Associates: 24 (center), 48 (left), 72, 84, 85, 86 (bottom right)
Superstock International Ltd.: © E. Streichen, cover, 92, 78; © O.J. Troisfontaines, 90
UPI/Bettmann Newsphotos: 31
Valan: © Aubrey Diem, 11 (left), 43
Len W. Meents: Maps on 83, 90, 94, 97
Courtesy Flag Research Center, Winchester, Massachusetts 01890: Flag on back cover
Cover: View of Esch-sur-Sûre, Ardennes, Luxembourg

A picturesque old square in the town of Echternach

TABLE OF CONTENTS

Chapter 1   *The Mighty Mite* (An Introduction) 7

Chapter 2   *The Crossroads of Europe* (History to 1868) 15

Chapter 3   *War, Peace, and a Second War* (History from 1890 to the Present) 25

Chapter 4   *Iron and Steel* 37

Chapter 5   *An Industrial Nation* (Commerce, Industry, and Employment) 45

Chapter 6   *Forests, Farms, and Vineyards* 55

Chapter 7   *Living in Luxembourg* 63

Chapter 8   *A Rich Culture* (The Arts, Communication, Transportation, and Holidays) 73

Chapter 9   *Villages, Towns, and the Capital* (A Tour) 83

Chapter 10   *The Grand Duchy, the European Community, and World Affairs* 101

Mini-Facts at a Glance 114

Index 122

Chapter 1

THE MIGHTY MITE

Luxembourg has been called the Home of the Brave, Europe's Green Jewel, and the Green Heart of Europe. Sometimes it is called Mighty Mite. Luxembourg is all of these and more.

Tiny Luxembourg claims only 998 square miles (2,586 square kilometers). But, despite its size, Luxembourg is a country of economic importance. The capital city of Luxembourg, called Luxembourg City or simply Luxembourg, is the headquarters of many national and international institutions. Almost one-fifth of the country's population lives in the capital.

The Grand Duchy of Luxembourg is located in western Europe. In 1921 it joined with Belgium in an economic union. Later it became a part of the Benelux, an economic union of Belgium, The Netherlands, and Luxembourg. It is now a member, with fourteen other Western European countries, in the European Union.

Less than 5 percent of the working population is engaged in agriculture. Mechanization still does not enable farmers to produce enough food for the Luxembourgers and foreigners who live in this small country.

Opposite page: Luxembourg City

A woman picking grapes in a vineyard

THE PEOPLE

Luxembourgers are very proud of their country. Some paint their country's national motto, *Mir welle bleiwe wat mir sin*, on their houses. Translated, this motto means, "We want to remain what we are."

The tiny principality is bordered by France on the south, Belgium on the west and north, and Germany (the Federal Republic of Germany) on the east. However, it maintains its own national and social character. Overrun by the armies of many nations, the people have retained their identity

At home the people speak Letzebuergesch, a tongue belonging to the Germanic language group. But, French and German also are spoken. All three—Letzebuergesch, French, and German—are official languages of the country

The Oesling area (left) is mountainous and the Gutland (right) has good farmland.

TWO REGIONS

Luxembourg can be divided into two regions on the basis of the physical characteristics of the land. Both contribute to its economy in distinct ways.

The northern third is known as the Oesling. The Oesling has beautiful highlands and the Ardennes Mountains that extend from southeastern Belgium and into part of Germany. The average altitude in the Oesling highlands is 1,250 to 1,600 feet (381 to 488 meters). The highest point is Buurgplaatz, with an altitude of 1,835 feet (559 meters), near the Belgian border.

The southern two-thirds are called the Gutland, which means the good land. The good farmland, many of the rivers, and most of the country's towns and villages are located in the Gutland. Ninety-one percent of the population lives in the Gutland, which includes Luxembourg City.

The forests, which cover about one-third of Luxembourg, have lovely streams, trails, and footpaths for hikers.

CLIMATE

Differences in wind direction and altitude in the Gutland and the Oesling produce different weather patterns in this country, which is a little smaller than the state of Rhode Island or about twice the size of Hong Kong.

The country's climate is described as temperate marine—cool and moist. There are no major differences in temperature and precipitation in the two sections of the country, however. The growing season in the Gutland is longer and the summers warmer than in the Oesling.

FORESTS, RIVERS, AND LAKES

Nearly one-third of the country is covered with forests. Where trees are harvested, reforestation is practiced. A dense forest, the Grunewald (Greenwoods) lies just three miles (five kilometers) outside Luxembourg City. There are many other forested areas with trails and footpaths for hikers.

The Moselle River (left) forms part of the border with
Germany. Vianden (right) lies in the Our River valley.

The country's most famous river is the Moselle, which forms
the southeastern border with the Federal Republic of Germany.
Luxembourg City was built at the confluence of the Alzette and
Petrusse rivers.

There are many other rivers in the country: the Our, Sûre, Syre,
Wiltz, Clervaux, and Blees. They provide opportunities for leisure
activities and sports.

Lake Sûre has been formed by a dam to provide drinking water
for a large area. Some electricity is also generated. There are
several other lakes where Luxembourgers enjoy recreation
throughout the year.

Campgrounds are filled with colorful tents and trailers.

OUTDOOR LIFE

Like many Europeans, Luxembourgers enjoy outdoor activities. Campgrounds are found along the rivers and streams and in the clearings in the woods. Colorful tents and campers dot the campgrounds. Residents and tourists enjoy hiking on sixteen national walking paths. Walking tours are organized over the weekends and on holidays. Hunting, fishing, boating, horseback riding, golf, swimming, and ice-skating are enjoyed.

THE CAPITAL

The Grand Duchy of Luxembourg is a constitutional monarchy, an independent sovereign state. The executive power is held by Grand Duke Jean and a Cabinet of twelve ministers.

The heart of Luxembourg is its capital. Ancient and modern exist side by side in one of the most picturesque capitals in the world. On the cliffs overlooking the Alzette and Petrusse river valleys, the modern city contrasts with the fortifications built along the valley walls a thousand years ago.

The capital is an international financial center and the location of RTL, Radio-Tele-Luxembourg, which broadcasts daily to forty million people throughout Europe.

In the Grunewald, northeast of the city, are some new buildings of the European Union. Three months of the year the Council of Ministers of the European Union meets in Luxembourg. The Court of Justice and other juridical bodies of the European Union are here also.

A COUNTRY AT PEACE

Luxembourg has been the crossroads of Europe for two thousand years. Many groups have invaded the country and fought to control it through the centuries. Its last bitter encounter came in World War II, when it was occupied by the Nazi army.

The constitution guarantees the citizens freedom of the press, religion, assembly, opinion, and trade and industry.

The country has a low unemployment rate, low inflation, and a high standard of living. It is a strong, stable democracy, a mighty mite matching much larger countries in per capita productivity.

Julius Caesar (left) sent his armies to conquer the land that is now Luxembourg. Remains of a Roman villa (above) were found near Echternach in the 1970s. The National Museum (below) contains artifacts from early settlements.

Chapter 2

THE CROSSROADS
OF EUROPE

PREHISTORIC SETTLEMENTS

People have lived in the part of Europe that we now call Luxembourg for many thousands of years. Archaeologists have found stone and bone tools from the Paleolithic Period of over twelve thousand years ago. A skeleton from the Mesolithic Period before 5000 B.C. was found near Reuland northeast of the capital. There are evidences of prehistoric Neolithic settlements in the Gutland.

During the Bronze and Iron ages many settlements existed, especially in the Moselle region in the south. The National Museum has exhibits of items from these periods.

Later the Celts from eastern France and southwestern Germany moved in. Although there were many tribes, they were united in their Druidic faith. The Celts raised livestock, farmed, and were good craftsmen.

JULIUS CAESAR CONQUERS GAUL

The Roman general, Julius Caesar, sent his legions into Western Europe, which the Romans called *Gallia* or Gaul. Gaul stretched from the Alps to the Atlantic Ocean, from the Pyrenees Mountains and the Mediterranean Sea to the English Channel. Caesar conquered Gaul between 58 and 51 B.C. He divided Gaul into three parts, one of which included present-day Luxembourg. The Celts fought bravely but were finally defeated near a river, probably the Alzette near Luxembourg City.

Roman domination continued for over four centuries. The cultivation of grapevines, the introduction of fruit trees, and the expansion of trade were encouraged. Small farms dotted the countryside. On several occasions the Celts attempted to regain their independence, but they were unsuccessful.

THE CROSSROADS

The Romans recognized the strategic location of the area and traces of a Roman settlement and a fort still exist. When the Romans invaded the area, they built three main roads. The region became the crossroads of Europe. Two of the roads began in France, crossed the country, and met at Trier in Germany. One road came from Lyon and the other from Reims. A third road went up to Cologne, Germany. There also were many secondary roads.

THE FRANKS

In A.D. 406 the Franks from western Germany invaded the region. They occupied a large section of Luxembourg, especially around the Moselle River.

Christians began meeting in the German town of Trier in the fourth century. Christianity spread rapidly into Luxembourg. But

Clovis I was the first Germanic king to become a Christian.

the Franks abolished Christian worship when they conquered the area. In 481 Clovis I became king of the Franks. He was the first Germanic king to become a Christian and he encouraged the peasants to return to their religion. By 507 Clovis I had conquered most of Gaul, including present-day Luxembourg.

In 698 Willibrord, an Anglo-Saxon missionary, founded a monastery in Echternach, the oldest continuously occupied settlement in the country. Echternach became not only a religious center but an art center as well.

CHANGES

The Franks introduced a new language of Germanic origin out of which Letzebuergesch grew. Latin continued to have some importance in the region and in the thirteenth century an early form of the French language became important.

*The remains of
the castle that
Siegfried built
on the Bock*

COUNT SIEGFRIED

Through a deed issued by the Abbey of St. Maximin in Trier, Count Siegfried of the Ardennes acquired large landholdings around what is now Luxembourg City on April 12, 963. The land was near an old Roman fortress, Lucilinburhuc, and the road that ran from Paris to Trier. It included a fertile plain and the Alzette River.

Siegfried needed a center for his operations. He built another castle, the Lutzelburg, on the Bock, a rocky outcropping in the Alzette valley. Today it is in the center of Luxembourg City. Remains of his castle were discovered and opened to the public in 1963 on the one thousandth anniversary of his land acquisition. Fortifications built later had hidden it from view for many centuries.

The city, Lutzelburg, became the seat of government for the new country. From there the counts of Luxembourg ruled for almost two hundred years. The charter for the fortified castle, the town, and the country is still preserved in Trier, Germany.

Through succeeding centuries the counts of Luxembourg extended their land. Many Luxembourg knights joined the Crusades to the Holy Lands, but when they returned they were deeply in debt. Their lands also had suffered during their absence. Land was gained and lost by the sword.

In 1136, Conrad II, the last count of Luxembourg of the Ardennes, died. There were no male heirs. Consequently, the Holy Roman Emperor awarded the area to the House of Namur.

COUNTESS ERMESINDE TAKES OVER

Henri IV of Namur became the ruler and almost brought the area to annihilation. When he died in 1196, his daughter Ermesinde inherited claims she could not enforce. She was very young and needed protection. She married Theobald of Bar, a descendant of Count Siegfried's father Wigerik. After Theobald's death, Ermesinde married Waleran. Together they governed.

When Waleran died in 1225, Countess Ermesinde took over the government. She instituted many reforms and restored Luxembourg's prestige. She established schools, monasteries, and other primitive forms of social security and in 1244 extended individual liberties to the people. The citizens of Luxembourg City were granted personal freedom.

French became the official language. Through her marriages, as well as purchases, Countess Ermesinde peacefully increased the size of her country. Countess Ermesinde died in 1247, leaving a heritage of a unified Luxembourg. For many centuries the reforms she instituted remained.

Edward III (left) was the victor in the Battle of Crécy (above) in which John the Blind was killed.

A MIGHTY EMPIRE

Ermesinde's son and grandson, Henry I and Henry II, continued the work of their mother and grandmother. In 1308, Henry of Luxembourg was elected Henry VII, the first German emperor. Later he was elected emperor of the Holy Roman Empire. He was a wise administrator who hoped to bring all of Europe under a united rule.

Henry's son John succeeded him and reigned in Luxembourg for thirty years before losing his sight. When England invaded France, John came to the aid of his friend, Philip VI of France. Although he was blind, John asked to be led into the center of the battle. John the Blind was killed in the Battle of Crécy on August 26, 1346. Edward III of England, the victorious Black Prince, said, "The battle was not worth the death of this man." Edward took the three ostrich feathers from John the Blind's helmet and adopted the count of Luxembourg's motto, "I serve." The feathers and motto are still on the coat of arms of the Prince of Wales.

John the Blind, count of Luxembourg, is one of the country's national heroes. Under his leadership Luxembourg's influence

Charles IV

Philip the Good of Burgundy

was extended throughout Europe. Charles IV, John's son, succeeded him. He extended Luxembourg's influence even farther through Europe. By 1364, Luxembourg, which had become a duchy, was four times its present size. Under the succeeding two rulers, Luxembourg's glory passed.

OTHER MASTERS

Being at the crossroads of Europe meant that armies from surrounding countries could enter Luxembourg and attack the fortress on the Alzette River. Some of these attacks were successful, and for almost four centuries, foreign countries ruled in Luxembourg.

In 1443, Philip the Good of Burgundy brought the country under French rule. His troops found it impossible to capture the fortress. But a traitor led his soldiers up a secret path. They took the defenders by surprise and they were forced to surrender.

But one man, Jean Schalop, the mayor, fought the enemy single-handedly. Although he was overcome by the attackers, he is remembered as one of Luxembourg's heroes.

In the late fifteenth century when a descendant, Mary of Burgundy, married Maximilian, emperor of Austria, Luxembourg came under Austrian rule. In 1506, their son, Philip, married a Spanish princess, bringing the area under Spanish control. The country remained under Spanish rule until 1684.

When the Thirty Years' War began in 1635, once again the country became the crossroads of Europe. By 1659 the country lay devastated by the war and a plague. More than half of the population had died.

In 1684 the country was captured by the armies of Louis XIV of France. Fourteen years later Spain was again in control of Luxembourg after France ceded the area to Spain in negotiations.

The Golden Age of Luxembourg began in 1713, when The Netherlands and Luxembourg were forfeited to the house of Austria. Austrian rule lasted for over eighty years. Then in 1794, the French again laid siege to the fortress in the city. The Austrian garrison was starved out and the French gained control. Luxembourg was known as the Department of Forests. The French garrison left with the defeat of Napoleon in 1814.

THE GRAND DUCHY

The Treaty of Vienna in 1815 raised Luxembourg's status to a grand duchy. Despite receiving its autonomy, it remained a province under the king of The Netherlands. The country was forced to surrender part of its territory east of the Moselle, Our, and Sûre rivers to the Prussians. The Prussians sent a garrison to the fortress in 1815. They remained for fifty-two years.

In 1830, Belgium and Luxembourg revolted against the control of The Netherlands. The result was that, in 1839, the Walloon

The Treaty of Vienna was signed in 1815.

districts of the Grand Duchy were ceded to Belgium (now called the Belgium province of Luxembourg).

May 11, 1867 is an important date. The Treaty of London, signed by Germany, France, and other European nations, ordered Prussian troops to leave the Grand Duchy and demolish the fortress. A few gates, the remains of some towers, and the tunnels are all that survived. The treaty affirmed Luxembourg's freedom, territorial integrity, and neutrality. Jubilant Luxembourgers danced in the streets celebrating their independence.

On October 19, 1868 their charter announced to the world: "The Grand Duchy of Luxembourg forms a free state, independent, and indivisible." The people who had endured the rule of many countries had finally achieved their own identity.

Surrounded by powerful neighbors—Germany, France, and Belgium—Luxembourg is none of these, nor is it a mixture of the three. The country and its people have an entirely separate sense of national character.

This fort on the Bock (center) was used to protect Luxembourg City. During William III's (top) reign the neutrality of Luxembourg was recognized. Grand Duchess Marie-Adelaide (bottom) abdicated in 1919 in favor of her sister Charlotte.

Chapter 3

WAR, PEACE, AND
A SECOND WAR

After 1890 Luxembourg's ruler was William III, king of The Netherlands and grand duke of Luxembourg. His successors included Adolf I, William IV, and Marie-Adelaide.

The Treaty of London in 1867 established Luxembourg as a neutral, independent country. Germany had been one of the signatories of that treaty. But when World War I broke out, German military forces occupied the Grand Duchy. Germany ignored the terms of the treaty and Luxembourg was occupied from 1914 to 1918. Marie-Adelaide was the grand duchess at the time of the invasion.

WORLD WAR I

Perhaps it was inevitable that this country, the crossroads of Europe, should find itself again under foreign rule. Although Germany had signed the agreement guaranteeing Luxembourg's neutrality, Kaiser Wilhelm II ordered his troops to enter the Grand Duchy. On August 2, 1914, German troops invaded the country from Trier. Within twenty-four hours the country was completely occupied. The German army thus gained control over an important rail transportation route into France.

The Hague Convention of 1907 forbade armies to move troops, supplies, or munitions through neutral countries. Both Germany and Great Britain had signed a document guaranteeing Belgium's neutrality. However, on August 4, 1914, the German army marched into Belgium from Luxembourg. German headquarters were in Luxembourg. Their cavalry tore down the telephone lines and resorted to couriers to dispatch messages to the front.

More than three thousand Luxembourgers who volunteered for service with the Allies were killed. The Armistice was signed on November 11, 1918. On November 21 the United States First Division marched through Luxembourg City. General John Pershing, of the United States, appeared on the Grand Ducal Palace balcony with the Grand Duchess Marie-Adelaide.

By November 25 the German army had evacuated the country. The country had been devastated. But with typical Luxembourger determination, the population began rebuilding.

Soon after the end of World War I, dissidents called for the establishment of a republic. Their criticism was directed at young Grand Duchess Marie-Adelaide, who had succeeded to the throne in 1912. The dissidents claimed she had not demonstrated sufficient resistance to the German occupation authorities. On January 15, 1919, Grand Duchess Marie-Adelaide abdicated in favor of her sister Charlotte. (Marie-Adelaide died when she was twenty-nine years old.)

A plebiscite was held in September 1919 to decide if Luxembourg should become a republic with a president or remain a monarchy. Sixty-seven percent of the people voted to retain the monarchy. Grand Duchess Charlotte continued as the monarch.

Grand Duchess Charlotte

POLITICAL ADVANCES

Under Grand Duchess Charlotte, many social and political advances were made. In 1920 Luxembourg joined the League of Nations. In 1921 women were given the right to vote, and welfare and social security administrations were begun. That same year a customs and economic treaty was signed with Belgium. It permitted common customs tariffs, a common commercial policy, and a common currency, the Belgian franc. Luxembourg nevertheless retains its own currency.

In 1923 Luxembourgers erected a monument honoring those who were killed in World War I. It also confirmed the country's friendship with its allies. At the Paris and New York world fairs, the Grand Duchy had impressive exhibits. They demonstrated what a small country could achieve as a free nation.

In 1924 Grand Duchess Charlotte and Prince Felix were married. They were beloved and admired by their people. Under

German troops entered Luxembourg on May 10, 1940.

the leadership of the Grand Duchess Charlotte, the country's productivity and prosperity increased. For forty-five years she exercised executive power in war and peace.

WORLD WAR II

In 1939 the Grand Duchy again affirmed its neutrality. But this was ignored by Chancellor Adolf Hitler of Germany. On May 10, 1940, Luxembourg was invaded again. The Nazi German army marched in and overran the country within hours.

The royal family and government officials fled to France. From France they traveled through Spain to Portugal and on to London. There they formed a government in exile. In September 1941, Grand Duchess Charlotte, Prince Felix, the prime minister, and other officials went to the United States seeking assistance. Hereditary Grand Duke Jean visited Midwest cities where former Luxembourgers lived. A National Relief Fund was established in Chicago. On August 19, 1942, the members of the royal family were guests of President Franklin D. Roosevelt at the White House.

Citizens of Mersch watch as an American tank rolls into their town.

A few weeks later Hereditary Grand Duke Jean volunteered for service in the British army and Prince Felix joined the British Northern Command. Throughout the war, the royal family radioed messages of encouragement to their countrymen over the British Broadcasting Company. The morale of the people remained high despite great trials.

In August 1942, Germany declared Luxembourg a part of the Third Reich. Most Luxembourgers resisted. When the young men were conscripted for military service in the Wehrmacht, the people nailed their flags to their factories and went on strike. No amount of suffering imposed on the people could stop their determination to retain their identity as a nation. At least sixteen thousand people were arrested and sent to prison or to concentration camps for their resistance. The Gestapo rooted out those who refused to obey Nazi commands.

Thousands of young men fled and joined the British, Canadian, Free French, Free Belgium, and American armies. Still others assumed new identities so they could undertake reconnaissance missions for the Allies.

French, the country's official language at the time, was banned.

Officials tried to force all Luxembourgers to speak German, claiming it was their mother tongue. But the Luxembourgers maintained Letzebuergesch was their native tongue and insisted on retaining French also.

For centuries their country had been occupied by foreign armies. This time they were determined to maintain their identity at any cost. They paid dearly in forced labor, conscription, and imprisonment. With the enlistment of Prince Felix and Grand Duke Jean in the British army, the people were even firmer in their resistance.

In June 1944 Grand Duke Jean's regiment crossed the English Channel. In the Normandy invasion, the Allies moved across northern France and into Belgium. The British fought their way to the border where the grand duke crossed the Luxembourg frontier at Pétange. It was the place the royal family had left four years earlier when going into exile.

On September 10, 1944, the Luxembourgers rejoiced as Allied troops liberated the country. Prince Felix accompanied an American division on its march from Belgium to the capital. He had been in exile for over four years. Prince Felix and Grand Duke Jean appeared together on the balcony of the Town Hall. The people were jubilant.

THE WAR RESUMES

Generals George Patton, Omar N. Bradley, and H.S. Vandenburg of the United States set up their headquarters in the capital. War returned to Luxembourg.

Adolf Hitler declared to his generals that he would send his troops on an offensive through Luxembourg to Brussels and drove

American soldiers searching for land mines during the Battle of the Bulge

into Antwerp. Early on the morning of December 16, 1944, twenty German divisions with almost a thousand tanks crossed the Our River from Germany into the Ardennes of Luxembourg and Belgium. The attack line was sixty miles (ninety-seven kilometers) long.

Hitler realized that Allied troops would soon attack Germany's industrial center. He was determined to stage a last-ditch offensive. Only four weak American infantry divisions were in the region. Nevertheless the Americans fought heroically in bitter winter weather. At first thick fog prevented Allied planes from engaging in the battle.

The German divisions pressed forward in a surprise attack. They formed a great bulge in the defenders' lines and the Ardennes offensive became known as the Battle of the Bulge.

Some of the bitterest fighting took place around Bastogne, a Belgian town not far from the Luxembourg border. The town was surrounded. The German commander sent word to General Anthony McAuliffe to surrender. The general sent back a message: "To the German Commander: Nuts! The American Commander." His reply symbolized Allied resolve to fight on and win.

The Germans captured many Luxembourg towns. On December 19, a German parachute division captured Wiltz. The town was not recaptured until January 21, 1945. Clervaux was captured on December 17 and liberated on January 26, 1945. Vianden, taken on December 16, was the last town to regain its freedom—on February 12, 1945.

The Germans also drove toward Luxembourg City, but they did not succeed because of lack of supplies and fuel and strong Allied resistance. The Ardennes offensive failed. German troops were stopped before they could reach Brussels or Antwerp.

On February 13, 1945, enemy troops were again cleared from the Grand Duchy. By the end of the fighting, Americans suffered 81,000 casualties, of which 19,000 died. The British lost another 1,400. Winston Churchill called the Ardennes "the greatest American battle of the war."

It is no wonder that Luxembourgers remember their liberators with great affection in parades and celebrations every year. American flags fly alongside their own. Memorials especially to the American efforts on behalf of their freedom are found throughout the country. General George Patton is one of Luxembourg's heroes.

On April 14, 1945, Grand Duchess Charlotte returned triumphantly from exile. On September 10, 1945, a victory parade was held. British, American, Belgian, French troops—and three thousand men in the new Luxembourg army—participated.

Tributes to the Americans, who helped Luxembourg in World War II, include a statue of General George Patton (left) and an American tank beside a statue of an eagle (right) at Ettelbruck.

WAR'S DEVASTATION

When the war ended, 35 percent of the farmland could not be worked because of the devastation of the Battle of the Bulge in the Ardennes. The homes of sixty thousand people were rubble. One hundred sixty bridges and tunnels lay in ruins. Many miles of railway tracks had been torn up and removed by the Nazis. Railway engines and cars had been taken away.

The Germans had forced the Luxembourgers to operate their steel mills twenty-four hours a day, seven days a week. The mills were burned out from overproduction when the Nazis left. The workers were exhausted.

REBUILDING

People with less determination would have surveyed the ruins left by the war and despaired. But Luxembourgers had always

After World War II, roads and bridges were repaired and expanded.

known hard work. They resolved to rebuild as fast as possible.

The Allied governments had continued to recognize the exiled government throughout the war. When the country was liberated, the parliamentary institutions began work on reconstruction. A special tax was levied to assist in rebuilding. Within two years, even in the north and west that had been severely hit during the Battle of the Bulge, villages were rebuilt. Homes, farms, and churches were restored. Fields and vineyards were swept for land mines. Factories began production again. Roads and highways as well as the railway were not only rebuilt but expanded.

Fifteen years after the war, partial reparations were paid for the damage the German army had done.

THE MONUMENT TO NATIONAL SOLIDARITY

The National Monument of Luxembourg Solidarity was erected in Luxembourg City center at the end of the Viaduct of the

Passerelle, the first major bridge to be built in the city. It is situated on what was a cannon emplacement (Kanounenhiwwel) many years ago.

Patriotic feats in World War II, such as the general strike of August 30 and September 1, 1942, are embodied in its structure. The monument also depicts prison quarters as a reminder of the thousands who were imprisoned for their resistance to Nazi rule. An eternal flame burns at the base.

The monument was designed by the Luxembourg architect Rene Maillet and was dedicated in 1971. The beautiful stained-glass windows were designed by the Luxembourg artist Francois Gillen.

GRAND DUKE JEAN

Grand Duchess Charlotte abdicated in favor of her son, Hereditary Grand Duke Jean, who became grand duke on November 12, 1964. She was eighty-nine years old when she died on July 9, 1985.

A NEW ROLE

Linked since 1921 with Belgium in an economic union, Luxembourg also participates in the Benelux Economic Union, which includes The Netherlands and Belgium.

In 1948 Luxembourg gave up its neutrality when it joined various international political, economic, and military organizations. It became a member of NATO in 1949.

The Grand Duchy, at the center of Western Europe, was soon to gain importance far greater than it could ever have anticipated.

Inside a steel mill in Dudelange

Chapter 4

IRON AND STEEL

For hundreds of years, iron ore was mined in southern Luxembourg. The region is called the red earth basin. The iron-ore seam extended for fifteen miles (twenty-four kilometers) with a width of three miles (five kilometers) between Rodange on the west and Dudelange on the east along the French border. The most productive section of the red, iron-ore bearing rock was only two miles (three kilometers) long.

A LONG HISTORY

The Titelberg, a plateau between Differdange and Rodange, had been an important iron-ore mining region in Celtic times. The Celts were followed by the Romans who occupied the region for five hundred years. Archaeological digs have unearthed thousands of Roman coins from the first century B.C. to the fifth century A.D. But the Romans did not utilize the ore to any great extent.

By 1292, fortifications were built at Esch-sur-Alzette to protect Luxembourg from French attacks. In 1671 the fortifications were torn down. In the eighteenth century the town was known as "poor Esch," because of its low agricultural production.

All of this changed with the development of the iron and steel industry.

THE RED EARTH BASIN

Almost one-third of the country's population lives in the red earth basin. It is the industrial heart of the Grand Duchy. The open-pit mines changed the landscape. Now that the iron-ore deposits are mostly depleted, mining here has ceased and nature is reclaiming the region.

Esch-sur-Alzette, the second-largest city in Luxembourg, is located in this region. In 1841 this former Celtic settlement had a population of just thirteen thousand. Today the population is almost twenty-five thousand. It was even larger when the iron-ore mines were operating.

THE THOMAS PROCESS

The iron ore in the red earth basin was of poor quality because it contained great quantities of phosphorus. Iron and steel products made from the ore were brittle and weak. They could not be used in construction or machinery. It was essential to find a means of extracting the phosphorus from the ore.

In 1878, Sir Sydney Thomas and Percy Gilchrist, English engineers, discovered a method of removing almost all of the phosphorus from the iron ore. Luxembourg immediately obtained the rights to use the new process.

Two industries benefited from the Thomas process, as it was

Right: Sir Sydney Thomas, one of the engineers who discovered a method of removing phosphorus from iron ore. Above: The main street in Pétange

called. With the removal of the phosphorus, the iron and steel products could compete with those of other countries because the steel manufactured was no longer weak and brittle. Luxembourg became an industrialized nation and became an important steel producer until the demand diminished in the 1970s.

Agriculture was the second industry to benefit. The slag from the Thomas process is high in phosphorus. In a slag mill it is converted to fertilizer, available in bulk or packaged. Previously fertilizer had been too expensive for most farmers to use. With the addition of the phosphorus fertilizer, the soil in both the Oesling and the Gutland farms became more productive.

Within thirty years after the first steel mills began operation, the nation's economy changed. It had been based primarily on agriculture. Even though the new fertilizer increased agricultural production, the big change came in industrialization. Dudelange, Rodange, Differdange, and Pétange, together with Esch-sur-Alzette, formed the second urban concentration in the country.

ALMOST A CENTURY OF PROGRESS

The Differdange plant began production in 1897. In 1902 the mill began producing beams rolled through a process developed by an American inventor, Henry Grey. The plant was operated by a French and Belgian company. In 1967 it was merged with the steel producer named ARBED.

Until the phosphorus was removed from the ore, it was impossible to produce these beams. Tailor-made beams are produced at Differdange. They are used in building construction and the erection of giant towers in regions of earthquake activity. The beams meet the highest standards set by the United States, Great Britain and other European countries, and Japan.

Jumbo beams have been used in the construction of over sixty major skyscrapers in the United States in San Francisco, Los Angeles, Dallas, Houston, and New York. These jumbo beams may weigh 2,276 pounds (1,032 kilograms) per 3.3 feet (1 meter).

Bridges around the world have been built using the Grey beam rolling system. Bridges over the Seine and Rhine rivers were rebuilt with Grey beams produced at Differdange before World War II. These bridges helped the Allies advance to Berlin near the end of the war.

Differdange beams are used in many other construction projects, including drilling-rig platforms and tunnel construction. The tube mill at Differdange also supplies tubes for boilers and the petroleum industry.

IRON-ORE PRODUCTION

Rumelange was called "the red earth town." For almost a century it was the heart of the iron-ore mining industry. But in

The ARBED steel complex

1978 the last mine was closed. The former open-cast mines are covered with new vegetation. The entire region attracts tourists because of its beauty and its history.

A museum in an old mine at Rumelange is open to visitors. A little train carries visitors almost 200 feet (60 meters) underground where retired miners demonstrate both old and modern methods of mining.

The iron and steel industry became the foundation of the nation's prosperity. In 1974 Luxembourg reached its highest level of iron and steel production. Then the demand for iron and steel dropped during a worldwide recession, causing the steel industry's portion of Luxembourg's gross national product to fall from 26 percent in 1970 to less than 10 percent in 1978.

ARBED

A joint venture between two companies in 1871 was the foundation of the iron and steel industry in the Grand Duchy.

Four blast furnaces were constructed at Esch-Schifflange. In 1911, a third company joined the group. The result was ARBED, Aciéries Réunies de Burbach-Eich-Dudelange. Increased demand for steel resulted in the construction by 1912 of the first modern steelworks at Belval. It was known as the Adolf Emile works. It was taken over by ARBED.

In 1971 the blast furnaces at Esch-Schifflange were torn down and iron making ceased there. Today there are three blast furnaces at Esch-Belval that supply hot metal over a private track. Huge ladles hold a large supply of molten iron. Esch-Belval is the only iron making center in the country. It provides all of the Luxembourg melting shops with iron.

An extensive modernization program resulted in more efficient production of iron and steel products. It increased the workers' productivity, but decreased the number of jobs.

AN IMPORTANT INTERNATIONAL COMPANY

ARBED headquarters are in Luxembourg City. The ARBED group is one of the largest steel producers in Europe. It has modern plants in Belgium, Germany, and Brazil, in addition to Luxembourg. It employs a total of forty thousand people throughout the world.

About sixty percent of the employees at Differdange are Luxembourgers. Those remaining are mostly French and Belgian workers who enter the country each day. French, Belgian, and Italian workers are employed at Esch-Schifflange.

Since the recession in the 1970s, the work force at Esch-Schifflange has been reduced by 50 percent. Most of the reduction has come through retirement.

Much of the steel produced in Luxembourg is used as reinforcement in high-rise construction.

The mill at Esch-Schifflange produces reinforcing bars and rods used in concrete construction. These high-strength steel products meet national and international standards. The rod mill also makes fine drawn wire, welded mesh, bolts, rivets, nuts, chains, springs, and other products.

THE INDUSTRY'S EMPLOYEES

There are many different jobs in ARBED's mills. Many people work in production, shipping, construction, transportation, and sales. Others are employed in the laboratories and in developing new projects and products. Of great importance are the health department, quality control, and plant safety.

The "Circles of Quality" program at Differdange has given a feeling of personal responsibility to the employees. The plant's safety record is the best in the country's iron and steel industry. A special program provides a training center for students.

*ARBED, which has plants in Belgium, Germany, and Brazil
as well as Luxembourg, is one of the world's leading steel producers.*

IRON AND STEEL IN THE ECONOMY

ARBED has operated at a profit since 1984. It is organized into about fifty different companies worldwide.

Several hundred million tons of steel are used annually. But ARBED recognizes that substitute materials are replacing steel in some industrial products. It is important, therefore, to meet precise market needs in highly efficient manufacturing plants.

The iron and steel industry in Luxembourg, without coal mines and coke ovens to support it, still produces about four million tons annually. Now the iron ore comes primarily from the Lorraine region of France. Coke for the furnaces comes from the Saar region of the Federal Republic of Germany. More than 40 percent of the country's industrial workers are employed in the industry. Iron and steel provide almost 50 percent of Luxembourg's industrial exports. It also accounts for nearly 15 percent of the country's gross national product.

Through the iron and steel industry, Luxembourg has become a highly industrialized nation.

Chapter 5

AN INDUSTRIAL NATION

Prior to and following World War II, iron and steel production was Luxembourg's chief manufacturing industry. But agriculture was the country's main source of employment. Young people worked the family farm as they had for generations. Today less than 5 percent of the population is engaged in agriculture. Manufacturing, construction, and the banking industry now are the major employers.

THE IMPACT OF STEEL

Postwar Luxembourg found itself with a devastated iron and steel industry. However, the industry recovered. The best years for the industry were from 1946 to 1974.

After the demand for Luxembourg's steel declined, ARBED began a modernization program at its mills. The government assisted the company by assuming part of its debt. Modernization and improvements have again made ARBED profitable. The government owns one-third of the company.

ADJUSTING TO CHANGE

Although the number of employees has decreased, the mills have increased productivity. The residents in the red earth district have learned to adjust. In a small country, what affects one region affects the entire country. Pétange and Rodange have organized an industrial zone to attract a number of manufacturing companies to the area.

Luxembourg has encouraged the development of other industries. A 1962 law that permitted foreign investment has been renewed. By 1986, 140 new firms had been opened. Seventy-five of these new firms were created in the ten years between 1976 and 1986. The 140 firms employed over 15,000 persons.

Many young people in the Oesling sought employment in the manufacturing plants instead of remaining on the family farms. Although these farms are highly productive, the young people wanted to improve their standard of living. Industry in the Oesling, the northern third of the country, is almost nonexistent. The canton of Clervaux, the most northern region, has faced economic problems not unlike those in the mining district.

AN INDUSTRIAL REVOLUTION

Some of Luxembourg's former industries have been revived. Leather tanning once had been an important activity, and now the industry is being revived. For over a thousand years, Wiltz has been the center of the leather industry. The export of hides and leather goods has increased in the past fifteen years.

Stone, glass, and ceramic products have become important in the export market. In 1974 they provided only a small part of the

Pottery beer steins on display in a shop window

country's exports. The excellent quality of Villroy and Bosch ceramics has made them popular in markets throughout the world. By 1986 the products were worth seven times what they had been in 1974.

For many years the village of Nospelt was a pottery-making center. Today the handicraft has been revived as both a profession and a hobby. Every Easter Monday potters set up stands to sell their handicraft. Hundreds of visitors come to the village as the people honor the patron saint of potters. A favorite souvenir is a pottery whistle in the form of a bird, called *peckvillchen*.

FOREIGN INVESTMENTS

Luxembourg offers a favorable climate for foreign investments. Luxembourg's factories operated at 85 percent of capacity in 1986.

A textile mill (left) and a General Motors automobile plant (right)

New plants in medium and light industry are the result. American investments include a Goodyear tire factory at Colmar Berg. The factory employs over thirty-six hundred people. Built in 1951, the factory was expanded in 1983. Goodyear is one of the largest private employers in Luxembourg.

Other American companies include General Motors; DuPont chemicals; Guardian Industries, which produces glass; National Intergroup, which makes aluminum foil; Monsanto; and Commercial Shearing.

In 1988 the United States air force started construction on a reserve hospital at Echternach. The development of a medical treatment and research center at Mondorf was under consideration.

Great Britain, Germany, France, and Belgium also have important investments in Luxembourg.

Foreign investments in medium and light industry have been welcomed by the Grand Duchy. The government offers incentives in taxes, construction, and plant equipment. Luxembourg enjoys peaceful labor relations. Unions are linked to one of the political parties. Representatives of employers, labor unions, and the government conduct labor negotiations. These excellent labor relations are a prime reason for many foreign investors locating in the Grand Duchy.

THE COUNTRY'S EXPORTS

Three-fourths of Luxembourg's exports go to the other fourteen member countries in the European Community. Belgium and the Federal Republic of Germany are the Grand Duchy's chief trading partners. The United States accounts for about 5 percent each of the country's exports and imports.

Steel is the country's most important export. Member countries in the European Community purchased 75 percent of the output in 1986 and the United States imported 4 percent. Most of ARBED's production and sales are controlled by quotas set by the European Union commission.

Luxembourg exports chemicals, glass, aluminum products, plastic containers, and rubber goods—especially tires. Imports and exports of textiles, furniture, toys, and sports equipment are almost equal.

Neighboring countries buy Luxembourg beer and wine. Some years the grape harvest and the wine produced is less than expected, but the quality is nevertheless excellent.

IMPORTS

Luxembourg is an attractive market. It has a very high per capita income and depends on imports to supply many of its needs. The country spends more for its imports than it collects for its exports. Its own economic well-being depends on the economic strength of its trading partners. When steel exports decline, the economy is negatively affected.

Belgium, France, and Germany have much larger markets than their small neighbor. Their importers and distributors have representatives in Luxembourg.

Eighty percent of Luxembourg's imports come from European Union countries. Mineral products, mechanical and electrical equipment, metals, and consumer goods dominate imports. The country imports less than 5 percent of its consumer and industrial goods from the United States. This contrasts with more than 30 percent each from Belgium and Germany.

Luxembourg's value-added tax of 6 to 12 percent is one of the lowest in Europe. Shoppers from nearby countries travel to the Grand Duchy to take advantage of lower prices for consumer goods. American food specialties sell well in the supermarkets.

Luxembourg has a trade deficit every year. It imports more than it exports. But a surplus of a billion dollars annually results from revenue in its banking and financial services.

A FINANCIAL CENTER

Like Switzerland, Luxembourg is a major financial center. Next to the steel industry, banking is the most important sector in the

The National Savings Bank in Luxembourg City

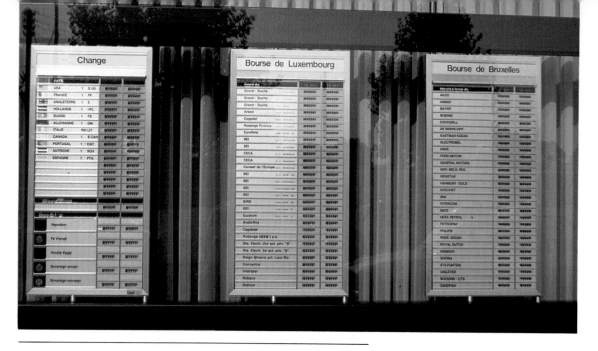

International financial information is posted in a bank window.

economy. Eight percent of the working population is employed in the banking industry.

Early in the 1980s the government began a program promoting growth in the financial sector. The country's location in the heart of Europe, political stability, employees who speak several languages, and excellent telecommunications attract foreign investors. Investments are attractive in Luxembourg. Low tax rates, subsidies, and financial assistance are made to companies engaged in research and development.

There are 218 international banks in the city. Eighteen thousand people were employed in the banking industry in 1993. Total deposits were over 60 million francs. Eighty-five percent of the deposits are in foreign currencies. Germany has the largest number of banks in Luxembourg. Scandinavian, Japanese, and American banking institutions rank next. Banks from many other countries are represented.

The capital is also the center for seventy insurance corporations, over four hundred mutual investment funds with a total deposit of $356 billion, and eleven thousand holding companies.

EMPLOYMENT AND INFLATION

Luxembourg's unemployment rate was 2.4 percent in late 1994. Of the 165,000 persons in the work force, 37 percent are non-Luxembourgers. About 120,000 persons living in Luxembourg are foreigners. They include Portuguese (8 percent), Italian (6 percent), Belgian, French, German, Spanish, and other nationalities. Many are employed in the banking and insurance industry and the offices of the European Union or foreign firms. Many of the Portuguese work in the iron and steel mills. In the capital, the percentage of foreigners is 38 percent, but countrywide it is 32 percent.

Foreign workers and their families living in Luxembourg often have difficulty being absorbed into the country's culture. There are frequently language barriers and local customs are unfamiliar to new residents. The government is developing programs to alleviate these problems.

Radio and television programs are frequently broadcast in other languages to accommodate foreign residents.

Many workers employed in manufacturing and in the iron and steel industry live across the border and enter Luxembourg each morning. When their work shift is over they return to their homes in their own countries.

The country's inflation rate was around 3.3 percent in 1993. Annual economic growth exceeds 2 percent.

Although it must import many raw materials and finished products demanded by a modern society, Luxembourg enjoys one of the highest standards of living in the world.

The "Little Switzerland" region of Luxembourg

Chapter 6

FORESTS, FARMS, AND VINEYARDS

A VERY SMALL COUNTRY

The country of Luxembourg is only one-fourth the size it was in A.D. 1250. It is only 55 miles (89 kilometers) from north to south and 35 miles (56 kilometers) from east to west. The country's shape is irregular. Its border with France is 43 miles (69 kilometers); with Germany, 81 miles (130 kilometers); and with Belgium, 89 miles (143 kilometers).

FORESTS

Forests cover the Oesling, the northern third of the country. The hills are a continuation of the Ardennes, which extend through part of northeast France, southeast Belgium, and part of Germany.

The beautiful German-Luxembourg National Park covers 283 square miles (733 square kilometers) on either side of the Our and the lower Suyvre rivers. The region is sometimes called "Little Switzerland." Near Echternach there are sandstone formations. The natural park has become a favorite recreation area for people of many countries. It is also just a pleasant place for a drive, especially in the autumn when the leaves have turned to russet and gold.

About 31 percent of the "Green Heart of Europe," as Luxembourg often is called, is forested. Oak, Norway spruce, pine, fir, birch, beech, and other species of trees abound. In the Ardennes, where trees have been cut down for lumber, many acres are being reforested.

Just three miles (five kilometers) outside Luxembourg City lies a dense forest called the Grunewald. The many trails and footpaths make this area a favorite region for hikers.

In autumn Luxembourgers enjoy Indian summer, when the leaves of the trees in the forests take on a beautiful hue. Deer, wild boar, and an occasional wildcat live in the forests and are among the few wild animals in Luxembourg.

Some timber is cut for domestic use. Only a small portion is exported. Instead, Luxembourg must import large quantities of wood and cork. The bark of the oak trees is stripped and used for tanning leather.

CLIMATE

Differences in altitude between the Oesling and the Gutland produce different local climates. Although the country's climate is described as temperate marine, there are great differences in temperature and precipitation in various sections.

Luxembourg is 200 miles (322 kilometers) from the sea. The sea winds from the northwest and southwest lose some of their moisture before they reach the country's border. Nevertheless the Ardennes-Oesling region has considerable rainfall and cold winters with often heavy snows and a late spring.

The climate in the Gutland is milder. The southerly winds are warmer. There also is a drier easterly wind. Summers are warmer and the growing season is longer than in the Oesling.

The average afternoon temperature in the country ranges from thirty-six degrees Fahrenheit (two degrees Celsius) in January to seventy-four degrees Fahrenheit (twenty-three degrees Celsius) in July. But temperatures in the two regions vary with altitude and aspect.

FARMS

At the Treaty of London in 1867, Luxembourg was guaranteed its neutrality as well as its independence. With characteristic dedication, the people worked very hard.

The country was impoverished, however. Although Luxembourg was important strategically, it was poor. Agriculture was the chief industry. But the farmers could not produce enough food to feed the growing population.

The birthrate had greatly increased by 1860. Originally the eldest son inherited the family farm upon the death of the father. The other children had to learn trades, join a foreign army, or enter religious orders. The young women could marry a farmer, sometimes in another village, move to the cities, or remain single.

Then a law regarding land inheritance was instituted. A farm had to be divided among all of the children when the father died. The Luxembourgers adopted this law. Within two generations, farms in Luxembourg were so small they could not support a family.

In one debate in Parliament, it was reported that farmers had only milk, bread, and potatoes to eat. Laborers were fortunate if they had meat twice a week.

Farming was difficult in the Oesling. The soil was poor. In the Gutland, much better harvests were realized. Both regions, however, needed fertilizer to increase production.

EMIGRATION

The farms were so small that farmers could not prosper. Many owners of small farms sold their land to their neighbors. But it was difficult for them to find other work.

Entire families emigrated to other countries. Some bought more land then they could ever hope to own in Luxembourg. In the United States, the Homestead Act helped the immigrants obtain land in new regions.

Luxembourg craftsmen faced many problems too. Industrialization in other countries resulted in products that were cheaper to produce than those in Luxembourg. The skilled shoemakers, cabinetmakers, tailors, and other craftsmen could not compete with machine-made products. Unable to find work in neighboring countries, many of them, too, emigrated.

The first Luxembourg immigrants in America sent letters telling about the abundance in their new homes. They stressed political freedom and the chance for advancement. Steamship lines offered reasonable fares. Often those who came to America paid the fare for other relatives to emigrate later.

By 1889, between thirty-five and forty thousand Luxembourgers had emigrated to America. Iowa, Minnesota, and Illinois received the largest numbers. Even today some people say there are more Luxembourgers or people of Luxembourg descent in Chicago, Illinois, than in Luxembourg itself.

The immigrants worked hard and prospered in their new

Farming has become more efficient, although the number of farms has decreased.

country. They retained their pride in their homeland, forming musical and choral societies. Although they spoke Letzebuergesch at home, the children soon learned English.

FEWER FARMS PRODUCE MORE

Meanwhile in Luxembourg, the number of farms decreased. Since 1960, the total area under cultivation has gradually dropped from 349,228 acres (141,329 hectares) to 150,000 acres (60,705 hectares) in 1992. But farming is more efficient and the kinds of crops grown have changed.

After the adoption of the Thomas process, the by-product of the steel industry was phosphorus. With the addition of phosphorus fertilizer, the soil became more productive and farm production increased dramatically.

A farmer using a horse-drawn plow (left). A worker loads bales of hay onto a wagon (right).

Farms have increased in size and mechanized equipment is widely used. In 1950, there were few harvester threshers. By 1972 the number had risen greatly on larger farms. Although there are still many horses on farms, the number of tractors has multiplied six times in the past few decades. Animal fodder, grains, and root vegetables are the principal farm products. Under the Common Agricultural Policy, farmers are guaranteed a specific price for certain crops. This is one of the results of cooperation in the European Union.

In the past twenty-five years, the number of livestock also has increased. So has the production of milk, butter, and cheese, as dairy farming has become more important. In 1992, there were over 209,000 cattle in the Grand Duchy. Seventy thousand pigs, as well as poultry and sheep, are raised on some farms.

Vineyards along the Moselle River

VINEYARDS

Luxembourg's vineyards and those of Great Britain are in the most northerly grape growing areas in the world. Grapes have been grown in Luxembourg since Roman times.

The slopes along the Moselle River facing southeast on the country's eastern border have many miles of vineyards. More than 3,250 acres (1,315 hectares) are covered with vineyards. Most of the wine that is produced is a high-quality white wine. Each bottle carries the national mark, which guarantees its quality. Most of the production is sold at home, although some wine is exported, especially to Belgium and The Netherlands. Luxembourg imports wine from France and Italy.

Chapter 7

LIVING IN LUXEMBOURG

Luxembourg has a 100 percent literacy rate. One of the national tongues, Letzebuergesch, is unique to Luxembourg. It was adopted as a national language in 1939. Most of the time, Luxembourgers speak Letzebuergesch. It is not usually used as a written language, but an oral one—one that very few foreigners understand. There is a strong national pride in Letzebuergesch. It is a phonetic language that is difficult to use in written communication.

Most Luxembourgers are trilingual. They are fluent in Letzebuergesch, French, and German, their official languages. Letzebuergesch is used in the home. German is taught in the elementary schools and French in the secondary schools. English is offered in the school curriculum also. Many people understand and speak English. Many also understand Portuguese, Spanish, and Italian.

The country's five newspapers are printed in German, although many articles are printed in French and occasionally in English and Letzebuergesch.

French is used in the courts, law, and civil service. German is the language in criminal law proceedings. The Parliament uses all three official languages in its debates and proceedings.

Opposite page: A flower market in Luxembourg City

Teenagers at a bus stop

EDUCATION

About 13.3 percent of public expenditures goes to education.
Primary school education is compulsory and free in state-run
schools for children from ages six through fifteen. There are over
five hundred primary schools for the twenty-six thousand
primary-level students. Nursery schools, many of them private,
enroll over eight thousand pupils beginning at two years of age.

About eleven thousand students from twelve to eighteen years of
age attend secondary and technical schools. The secondary schools
are like the gymnasiums of Germany and the lycées of France.
They are state supported, but there may be a small tuition charge.
There also are agricultural institutions and vocational training
schools.

A primary school in Vianden

The Superior Institute of Technology enrolls over three hundred students in higher education. In the 1960s, the International University of Comparative Sciences, with major studies in law and economics, opened.

About twenty-five hundred secondary-school graduates attend universities in other countries, especially in France, Belgium, and Germany. They receive degrees in many different subject areas.

With so many families from other countries working in the offices of the European Union in Luxembourg City, two private schools have been opened. One is the American International School for English-speaking children from kindergarten through twelfth grade. The other school, the European School in Kirchberg, is operated by the European Union.

RELIGION

More than 95 percent of the population are declared Roman Catholic; almost two-thirds of the people are practicing Catholics. Luxembourg's constitution guarantees freedom of religion. Two Protestant churches and a Jewish synagogue are located in the capital. Priests, Protestant pastors, and the Jewish rabbi are paid by the state.

Schools, hospitals, and retirement homes run by the churches and staffed by nuns are supported in part by the state.

HEALTH

Life expectancy in the Grand Duchy is 72 years for men and 79 years for women. Health insurance is provided for illnesses, industrial accidents, and family services. A small charge is made for visits to doctors and the hospital. There are over eight hundred physicians and over four thousand hospital beds in the country.

A DECLINING BIRTHRATE

The number of Luxembourgers is dropping, while the number of foreigners living in the country is increasing. Luxembourgers accounted for 74 percent of the population in the country in 1986. For every 1,000 Luxembourgers, 13.4 children are born annually. For foreign residents, the birthrate is 14.8 per thousand. The world average is 25 per thousand. The government is concerned about the decreasing birthrate.

Outdoor cafés and restaurants are popular for dining or just people watching.

FOOD AND THE CULINARY ARTS

Luxembourgers are known for their appreciation of fine food, good wine, and locally made beer. The cuisine, or style of cooking, is influenced by both France and Germany. Hearty meals are traditional—an influence of Germany's ample portions.

Favorite dishes include *judd mat gaarde-bounen*, smoked pork and beans or sauerkraut; *jambon d'Ardennes*, Ardennes ham; *quenelles de foie de veau*, liver dumplings; and, during the hunting season, *civet de lièvre*, hare in a thick sauce. *Cochon de lait en gelée*, suckling pig in aspic, and *fleeschtaart*, a meat pie with minced pork, also are served. Many of these are Luxembourg specialties.

From April 1 to September 30, crayfish and trout served Luxembourg fashion, and fried pike and small fish from the Moselle, Sûre, and Our rivers are favorites.

Volleyball is a favorite sport.

Special pastry shops display delicious sweets for desserts. On Shrove Tuesday, people buy a cake called *les pensées brouillées,* "random thoughts." Plum cake is a special treat in September.

In the Middle Ages beer was brewed in the monasteries. Today modern breweries use the latest equipment and produce first-class beer. The quality of its wines is monitored by a quasi-state institution, the Office of Luxembourg National Registered Wines. There are many white wines from which to choose.

RECREATION AND SPORTS

Luxembourgers enjoy the outdoors. Although it may be only a short distance from their homes, they drive campers or pitch their tents in the country's many campgrounds. Young people stay at youth hostels. Boy Scouts and Girl Guides use special chalets and campgrounds without charge. The grand duke is chief scout of the Luxembourg Boy Scout Association. Scouts from other parts of the world gather at Wiltz each summer.

A young cyclist takes a break

Luxembourg has many marked hiking trails. People of all ages find pleasant walks and hikes healthy activities. There are sixteen national hiking routes marked with yellow signs. They total 372 miles (598 kilometers) and are found in scenic areas throughout the country. The Youth Hostel Association has trails marked with white triangles between all of the youth hostels.

There are many other walking paths and trails. Nearly every Saturday, Sunday, and holiday, walking tours are organized on special trails from six miles (ten kilometers) to twenty-four miles (thirty-nine kilometers) in length.

Cycling is also a favorite sport. Several specially marked trails are available and there are plans to increase them.

A glider center is located at Useldange. Visitors are welcomed from May 1 to the end of October to enjoy a ride or watch the gliders take off and land.

Fishing in the Sûre River at Esch-sur-Sûre

Many Luxembourgers who enjoy active sports play tennis, soccer, squash, or volleyball. Hunting, fishing, swimming, canoeing, and boating are popular. Cross-country skiing is available, weather permitting, in three places. Two towns have rinks for ice-skating.

The grand duke is the honorary president of the Luxembourg Olympic Committee and a member of the International Olympic Committee. Luxembourg had participants in the 1988 Olympic games.

People enjoy meeting their friends at small cafés. Often chess matches are held in the cafés and restaurants.

A beautifully landscaped home in Vianden (left) and a house with a built-on barn in the Ardennes region (right)

STANDARD OF LIVING

Sixty percent of Luxembourgers own their homes. In the capital and some of the larger towns, many people rent apartments. In small towns, on farms, and in rural areas, homes are owned by the occupants.

Traditional farm cottages are thick-walled and well built with heavy beams and provide comfort and modern conveniences. There also are palatial homes and, of course, dozens of medieval castles.

The Luxembourg standard of living, as judged by automobile ownership, television sets, and telephones, is the highest in the European Union. Every house has electricity.

In terms of its inhabitants' standard of living, Luxembourg ranks among the richest countries in the world. Workers travel only short distances to and from work. There is time to enjoy the country's beauty and recreational facilities.

The Cathedral of Notre Dame in Luxembourg City

Chapter 8

A RICH CULTURE

Many countries have contributed to Luxembourg's culture over more than two thousand years. However, the Grand Duchy has developed its own artistic style. Its art, architecture, literature, and drama are uniquely its own.

REMEMBERING THE PAST

Luxembourgers treasure their rich heritage. They also treasure their independence. In 1941, Adolf Hitler ordered a referendum seeking approval to incorporate the country into the Third Reich. Overwhelmingly the Luxembourgers voted against it. At no time was their resolve, "We want to remain what we are" more evident. They chose to retain their culture despite heavy penalties.

ARCHITECTURE

Archaeologists have uncovered remains of the cultures of Celtic and Roman times. Monuments, villas, and palaces built almost two thousand years ago have been found.

The Cathedral of Notre Dame in the capital is a beautiful example of Gothic architecture. The Grand Ducal Palace, which

The Municipal Theater

dates in part from the sixteenth century, was built in the Italian Renaissance style. It originally served as the town hall.

Since World War II, modern structures have been built. A new Municipal Theater, designed by a French architect, was opened in 1964. It was built to commemorate the one thousandth anniversary of Luxembourg City. The materials and services of many European communities were used to construct the two halls and the foyer where receptions are frequently held.

In many towns and villages, homes, churches, and other buildings have been rebuilt since World War II. Buildings in the capital are a mixture of traditional and modern structures. The modern steel-and-glass buildings house many of the offices of the European Union. New hotels have been built in Luxembourg City and close to modern Findel International Airport, east of the city.

A stunning stained-glass window dominates the railroad station in Luxembourg City.

THE ARTS

The arts are encouraged in Luxembourg, although the works of other European artists are displayed as well as those of Luxembourgers.

Daniel Muller, one of the country's great sculptors, prepared the portals and screen in the art gallery in the early seventeenth century.

The works of Luxembourg artists Joseph Kutter, an impressionist; Jean-Pierre Beckius; Dominique Lang; Berthe

*The National Museum exhibits the work of
international artists as well as historical artifacts.*

Brincour; and others are exhibited in the National Museum.

Among the most famous Luxembourg authors who wrote in
French are Felix Thyes and Marcel Noppeney. Those who wrote in
German include Nikolaus Welter and ''Batty'' Weber. Michael
Rodange, who lived in the nineteenth century, wrote in his native
language, Letzebuergesch. The country's greatest poet was Paul
Palgen.

NEWSPAPERS

Luxembourg's five daily newspapers have a circulation of over
146,000. The most widely read is *Luxemburger Wort* (*Luxembourger*

Voice) published in German and French. Some articles are printed in both languages. Occasionally there are articles in English and Letzebuergesch. *Tageblatt*, published in German, has the second-largest circulation.

RADIO LUXEMBOURG, RTL, AND FILMS

The Luxembourg Radio Broadcasting Company, a private enterprise, was established in 1931. During World War II the Germans seized the radio station and broadcast Nazi propaganda. After liberation, the station resumed its own broadcasting on November 12, 1945. It is housed in a modern building with gardens, trees, and well-kept green lawns.

In 1945 the company was renamed Compagnie Luxembourgeoise de Telediffusion, RTL, and granted commercial television programming.

RTL radio programs are broadcast in French, German, English, Letzebuergesch, Dutch, Italian, Spanish, Portuguese, and Yugoslav. Television programs are in French and German. Forty million Europeans view or listen to RTL programs each week. Shortwave enthusiasts in the United States listen to the programs of CTL, the French initials of the company.

The company engages in other activities. There are over seventy musicians in the well-known RTL symphony orchestra. The orchestra gives fifty concerts annually in the Grand Duchy and other countries. The founder was Henri Pensis, a Luxembourger who studied in Germany. A music publishing company, other publishing firms, film productions, and a film rights department are part of RTL's activities.

Société Européenne des Satellites, a private company

Modern buses provide efficient transportation.

incorporated under Luxembourg law, launched a communications satellite, ASTRA, in 1988. The satellite is in a geostationary orbit to serve Western Europe. The control center is in Betzdorf, fifteen miles (twenty-four kilometers) from the capital.

TRANSPORTATION

With its location as the green heart of Europe, good roads are essential throughout the country to link it with its neighbors. There are 3,177 miles (5,113 kilometers) of roads. Of the country's over 208,847 automobiles, almost 40 percent were built in Germany and 18 percent in France.

Almost seven hundred buses serve the towns with fine transportation within the country and to other points in Europe.

The first railway line opened in 1859. By 1864 tracks were laid to link the country with its neighbors. The railways serve both passengers and freight. Rebuilt after World War II, there are 171 miles (275 kilometers) of track. With improved road transportation, the railway network has been reduced.

Since 1965 the Grand Duchy has been connected with the European waterway network through its port on the Moselle River at Mertert. Huge barges carry bulk freight.

Findel International Airport serves many foreign airlines as well as Luxair, the country's own airline. In 1991, almost 861,284 passengers landed at Findel International Airport.

HOLIDAYS

Luxembourg's national holiday on June 23 also is celebrated as Grand Duke Jean's official birthday. His actual birthday, however, is January 5. National Day is celebrated with a fireworks display in the capital on the eve of the holiday. Patriotic parades, religious services, and receptions are held throughout the country. Luxembourgers proudly display their solidarity on this day.

All Luxembourgers observe the country's legal national holidays. New Year's Day, Easter Monday, May 1, Ascension Thursday, Pentecost Monday, All Saints' Day (November 1), Christmas Day, and St. Stephen's Day (December 26) are national holidays in addition to June 23.

One legend relates that St. Nicholas descends from heaven on December 6 to bring presents to good children. On December 5, 1944, an American soldier dressed as St. Nicholas delighted the children of Wiltz with gifts of chocolate, pastry, and fruit collected from the troops' food rations when the town was liberated.

A religious procession

In the capital the solemn ceremony of the Octave of Our Lady of Luxembourg, which occurs after Easter, is the most important religious event of the year. People from all over the country make pilgrimages to pay homage to Our Lady of Luxembourg. The ceremony ends with a procession, complete with the statue of the Madonna, to various churches in parts of the city.

On August 24, St. Bartholemy's Day, a festival including the March of the Sheep is held in the city. Shepherds in traditional costumes drive their sheep through the streets.

When the broom, a bright yellow shrub, blossoms in May, Wiltz holds its Broom Parade, sometimes attended by Crown Prince (Hereditary Grand Duke) Henri.

Numerous fairs and festivals are held throughout the Grand Duchy with dancing, barbecues, and various amusement attractions.

Laying wreaths at a Remembrance Day ceremony

REMEMBRANCE DAY

Ettelbruck celebrates Remembrance Day on the first Sunday in July. Flags of the Allies fly with Luxembourg's red, white, and blue. People gather at the nine-foot (three-meter) statue of General George Patton. After wreath laying and the playing of the Luxembourg and American national anthems, the parade begins.

Luxembourg, American, Belgian, and French soldiers march behind camouflage-painted tanks. American air force fighter jets fly overhead, dipping their wings in tribute. Pétange also celebrates Remembrance Day.

A NATION'S TRIBUTE

Many towns exhibit reminders of the fierce fighting during the Battle of the Bulge. Monuments, especially in the north, plaques, statues, and even tanks are reminders of World War II.

Right: Ancient walls and gatehouses of Luxembourg City
Below: Upper and lower levels (left) and a viaduct over the Petrusse valley (right) in Luxembourg City

Luxembourg City

Chapter 9

VILLAGES, TOWNS, AND THE CAPITAL

The tiny principality of Luxembourg with its dense forests, deep valleys, winding rivers, charming villages, and dozens of castles that range from four hundred to more than a thousand years old is a visitor's delight.

LUXEMBOURG CITY

Of particular beauty is Luxembourg's capital city. It has become one of Europe's important meeting places. Its population, including its suburbs, is approximately 115,000. It is one of Europe's most interesting and historic cities.

Count Siegfried built his fortress on the Bock at the edge of a deep valley formed by the Alzette and Petrusse rivers. Three rings of city walls with fifty-three forts and strong points protected the city. Ten gates controlled entrance through the walls.

The Grand Ducal Palace in the Place Guillaume

Almost fourteen miles (twenty-three kilometers) of tunnels were blasted in the sandstone walls of the cliff above the Petrusse River for defense. The casements linked important points in the city's fortifications. Completed in 1746 by the Austrians, they provided a defense against invading French troops. The great defense system of Luxembourg City earned it the name ''Gibraltar of the North.'' Today city visitors enjoy touring the tunnels and casements where cannons once faced invaders.

The Grand Ducal Palace is close to the center of the old town. The oldest part, called the Spanish section, was built in 1572-73. Next to it is the building of the Chamber of Deputies, the Parliament, built in 1858-59.

The Cathedral of Notre Dame, with its three spires, was built in 1613-18. Beautiful works of art, the vault of the royal family with blue and gold mosaics, the sarcophagus of John the Blind, stained-

St. Michael's Church and castle are in the background.

glass windows, choir stalls, and the interesting doors add to the importance of this religious center. The Shrine of Our Lady of Luxembourg is the scene of the Octave, one of the most important religious observances in Luxembourg.

There are many other interesting churches in Luxembourg City. The Quirinus Chapel in the Petrusse valley, hewn out of rock in the fourth century, is one of the oldest shrines in Europe. The churches of St. Michael (1320) and St. John on the Rock are magnificent examples of religious architecture.

The National Library adjoins the cathedral. It contains over 600,000 books and 3,500 different periodicals and other publications. Thirteen thousand books were written by Luxembourg authors.

The National Museum has displays of paintings and works of art by foreign and Luxembourg artists, archaeological discoveries, and geological and historic exhibits in over one hundred rooms.

*Clockwise from above: A street
in the old part of the city,
an equestrian statue of
William III, and Pont Adolphe*

At the Place de la Constitution stands the memorial to the volunteers who fought for Luxembourg in World War I. The tall column held the statue of the goddess of Victory. The monument was destroyed by German forces in October 1940 during World War II. But Luxembourg workers salvaged the stone slabs and blocks and hid them in safe places. They vowed some day they would rebuild the monument. With love, they did restore their monument after the war.

There are 110 bridges in Luxembourg City. The most famous that span the deep, wide Petrusse valley are Pont Adolphe and Pont Passerelle. The Pont Grand Duchess Charlotte, which soars 280 feet (85 meters) over the Alzette valley, was completed in

Central Station, the train station, was completed in 1922.

1966. It links the city center with the section of the city housing institutions of the European Union.

Near the main railroad station is the modern section of Luxembourg City, with shops, banks, hotels, restaurants, and offices lining the four-lane Avenue de la Liberté. The most ancient area is a square called the Marché aux Poissons. Here are some lovely houses and the oldest café in the city.

There are so many historic and interesting places in this ancient-modern city that, despite its small area, visitors can spend many days exploring it. A tram ride in the Petrusse valley provides an orientation of its exciting history.

Approximately ten thousand soldiers are buried in the American Military Cemetery.

THE AMERICAN MILITARY CEMETERY

Near Hamm, just two miles (three kilometers) west of the city, is the American Military Cemetery. The people of Luxembourg purchased fifty acres (twenty hectares) of land and in 1951 offered it to the American people in gratitude for their liberation. The American government accepted the use of the land in perpetuity as a final resting place for American soldiers, including 101 unknown soldiers and airmen. Most of those who are interred died in the Battle of the Bulge in 1944-45.

A nondenominational chapel stands near the entrance to the cemetery. The Great Seal of the United States is carved above a dedication. On the other side is a dedicatory inscription in French and the Luxembourg coat of arms.

*General Patton's grave (left) and the German Military
Cemetery (right), which has about six thousand graves*

General George Patton, who is remembered with affection by
the people he helped to liberate, died in a traffic accident in
Germany after the war. He is buried near the men he commanded.
The cemetery lies in a peaceful circle of woods of beech, pine, oak,
and larch trees. Roses and lilacs bloom in the spring.

THE GERMAN MILITARY CEMETERY

At Sandweiler is the German Military Cemetery. Of the 11,000
German soldiers buried here, 4,829 lie in a common grave. Over
seven hundred are unknown. The cemetery was developed
through donations, much of it from German schoolchildren.

THE KIRCHBERG PLATEAU

A modern complex of buildings used by the European
Union has been erected on the Kirchberg Plateau just

The European Tower Building

outside the capital. Its twenty-two-story European Tower Building
was opened in 1966, a symbol of Luxembourg's commitment to
European integration. There are many new buildings in the
complex housing the offices of various commissions, the computer
center, Court of Justice, and European Investment Bank.

SOUTH OF LUXEMBOURG

With its over twenty-four thousand inhabitants, Esch-sur-
Alzette is the country's second-largest city. This capital of the
industrial district is just eleven miles (eighteen kilometers)
southwest of Luxembourg City. Its beautiful parkland and great
rose garden near the steel plants, along with its leisure and
cultural centers, and shopping areas attract many visitors.

The Resistance Museum has a collection of documents from the
period of German occupation from 1940 to 1945. A monument

A ferryboat crossing the Moselle River between Germany and Luxembourg

honoring the heroism of Luxembourgers during the occupation stands at the entrance.

Differdange with its population of sixteen thousand is the third-largest town in the country. Its steel mill produces the famous Grey beams and girders. Like Esch-sur-Alzette, it has an interesting cultural center.

THE MOSELLE VALLEY

Small settlements with populations of three hundred inhabitants or less lie along the Moselle River. A leisurely boat ride along the Moselle between Wasserbillig and Schengen provides an excellent view of vineyards, castles, and the river traffic.

The picturesque city of Clervaux

NORTH OF THE CAPITAL

In the Ardennes region, northeast of the capital, there are attractive towns with interesting histories. Clervaux, with its old castle and the Abbey of St. Maurice and St. Maur, is a charming tourist resort. There is little industry in Clervaux, so the present population of fourteen hundred receives income primarily from tourism.

Photographs taken by the famous American photographer Edward Steichen are exhibited in the castle. Steichen was born in Luxembourg.

The Luxembourg artist Michael Heintz produced the statue in the Memorial to the American GI on the Clerf River promenade. The Ardennes region had suffered greatly in the Battle of the

Views of Vianden include the castle above the town (above), a chair lift that transports visitors from the town to the castle (above right), and old buildings on a narrow street (right).

Bulge in December 1944. The statue was erected in honor of the 450,000 American soldiers who fought in the offensive.

Vianden, with only fifteen hundred inhabitants, is the capital of the largest tourist center in the country. Narrow streets lead past old houses and the churchyard has intriguing old tombs. The largest and best-restored castle in the country is open to visitors from April to November 1. The castle dates from the ninth century, but the magnificent additions were made in later centuries. A chair lift carries visitors up over 600 feet (183 meters) for a beautiful panorama of the town and the Our River valley.

Victor Hugo, the French author, lived in Vianden. The house in which he stayed is a museum. Vianden is the starting point and terminus of a footpath to Esch-sur-Sûre. Cycling, swimming, fishing, and canoeing are some popular outdoor activities.

Clervaux

Vianden

Esch-sur-Sûre

Luxembourg City

Scenes of Esch-sur-Sûre
clockwise from top:
The Sûre River, Upper Sûre Lake,
and a chapel among castle ruins

Many lovely villages are nestled throughout the countryside.

Esch-sur-Sûre, a lovely village of less than three hundred inhabitants, also is a popular tourist center. The Sûre River meanders through steep rock cliffs with the ruins of a towering castle in the village.

Campsites are popular along the Sûre. Outside the village a dam forms Lake Sûre. A power station produces electricity during the winter. The main reason for damming the river was to provide drinking water for the area.

THE HEART OF THE OESLING

Wiltz was invaded by Germany in 1940. Eight hundred of its one thousand houses were damaged or destroyed. The town was the center of the tanning industry.

There is a low section in Wiltz and then a section about 500 feet (152 meters) higher. Today it has several industrial plants, a health resort, and a college and school branches. It has become the economic center for the northern Oesling area.

Buildings of St. Willibrord Abbey in Echternach

Echternach on the bank of the Sûre has over four thousand citizens. Germany is across the river. Hundreds of footpaths crisscross the German-Luxembourg National Park. The region is especially beautiful.

St. Willibrord founded the Benedictine Abbey in the seventh century, which today contains primary and secondary schools. In the crypt of the basilica is the white marble sarcophagus of St. Willibrord. The crypt is decorated with frescoes from the eleventh century. Miracles have been attributed to St. Willibrord and

The town hall (left) and the Church of St. Peter and St. Paul (right), one of the oldest churches in the country, in Echternach

thousands come to honor him on Whitsuntide (the week beginning with Pentecost, the seventh Sunday after Easter).

The Church of St. Peter and St. Paul is the oldest sacred building in the town.

Echternach's International Music Festival in the summer hosts international symphony orchestras, artists, and musical groups. Excellent concerts are held in the basilica, the church, and other sites.

The castle of Vianden has been restored to its original plans.

Two-thirds of Echternach was destroyed in the Battle of the Bulge during World War II. Restoration began immediately after the war. The religious buildings have been returned to their former splendor.

The foundations of a palatial Roman villa were uncovered in 1975-76 to the south of Echternach. A mosaic floor, heated bathing area, and ornamental fountain have been excavated.

CHARMING VILLAGES

Luxembourg has been called a fairyland. And so it seems as one drives over well-paved roads with beautiful vistas at every turn. There are museums, medieval castles, beautiful valleys, and fascinating villages throughout the country. Paths along the rivers, simple villages with only a few hundred inhabitants, neat farms, and small churches with beautiful frescoes and altars lend a special charm to a country that has beauty in miniature.

The national motto, "We want to remain what we are," tells much about the character of the Luxembourgers. Their strength is in their faith and cultural development.

Above: An exterior view of the Vianden castle, which dates from the ninth century.
Below: The castle in Wiltz was built in the twelfth century and remodeled in 1631.

Chapter 10

THE GRAND DUCHY, THE EUROPEAN COMMUNITY, AND WORLD AFFAIRS

The Grand Duchy of Luxembourg is small in area. But in international affairs it plays a major role. It also is the only Grand Duchy in the world.

A CONSTITUTIONAL MONARCHY

During both world wars, the Allies recognized the Grand Duchy of Luxembourg as an independent state.

After many centuries of foreign rule, the country was made a Grand Duchy in 1815. Luxembourg dates its independence from 1839 when the Walloon district was given to Belgium and Luxembourg's frontiers were fixed, although it was not until 1867 that its independence and neutrality were formally guaranteed.

Luxembourg's constitution was written in 1839 and the last revision was adopted in 1956. The constitution assures the country of a representative democracy in a constitutional

Opposite page: The Grand Ducal Palace

monarchy. It provides for three branches of government: executive, legislative, and judicial.

THE EXECUTIVE BRANCH

The grand duke is the chief of state. Executive powers rest with the grand duke. He ensures that laws are enforced, administers public property, and affirms acts voted in the legislature. He nominates persons to serve in the consular corps. He also may initiate legislation.

The Council of Government (Cabinet) is headed by the president of the government. He is leader of the political party or coalition of parties having the most seats in the Chamber of Deputies. The grand duke formally chooses the president, who is generally called the prime minister. The vice-president of government is the leader of the party in the coalition with the second-highest number of seats.

In a national parliamentary election in 1994, the Christian Social party won a plurality. Jacques Santer became president and formed a coalition Cabinet. Cabinet officers administer various ministries covering all aspects of government affairs. In 1995, Santer took office as president of the Commission of the European Union (EU). Jean-Claude Juncker became prime minister, and a major reorganization of the Cabinet followed.

THE LEGISLATIVE BRANCH

Voting is held on a Sunday and is compulsory. Citizens who fail to vote are fined unless they have an adequate excuse.

Legislative powers belong to the Chamber of Deputies. Deputies are elected for five-year terms. The 1994 election resulted in a coalition government of twenty-one Christian Social party members and seventeen from the Socialist Workers party. The

The exterior of the Chamber of Deputies (left) and a meeting room inside (right)

opposition is composed of eighteen members from other parties.

There are sixty seats in the Chamber of Deputies, five having been added since 1979. Citizens vote according to their district: south, east, center, and north. Each deputy represents 5,500 citizens. Every session of the Chamber is opened or closed by the grand duke or an authorized representative.

Twenty-one members of the Council of State are appointed by the grand duke. They come from different sectors of society and serve as an advisory body. Their views are considered by the Chamber of Deputies in drafting legislation. The Council must deliver an opinion before a final vote can be taken on a bill.

Eleven members of the Council of State form the Disputes Committee. If citizens disagree with a decision made by the government, they can appeal to the Disputes Committee of the Council of State.

THE JUDICIAL BRANCH

Supreme Court members are appointed by the grand duke. The law in Luxembourg is derived from local practice, legal tradition, and the judicial systems of France, Belgium, and Germany. The Supreme Court is the top court in the judicial system.

LOCAL GOVERNMENTS

Aldermen, or burgomasters, in the municipalities are elected for six years. The burgomaster presides at municipal council meetings. District commissioners are links between the central government and the municipalities. They are appointed by the grand duke.

THE GRAND DUCHY

According to the pact of June 30, 1783, the crown of the grand duchy is hereditary in the Nassau family. The treaties of 1815 and 1867 affirmed this.

His Royal Highness the Hereditary Grand Duke Jean succeeded his mother, Grand Duchess Charlotte, when she abdicated in favor of him in November 1964. She had reigned for forty-five years. Grand Duchess Charlotte was beloved by her people. She had rejected neutrality when World War II broke out. Then when the German army invaded Luxembourg, she and officials of the government fled to London where they entered into an alliance with the Allies. After she abdicated in favor of her son, Grand Duke Jean, she lived long enough to see her country become an important member of the European Community.

Grand Duke Jean married Josephine-Charlotte, princess of

Belgium, on April 9, 1953. They have five children. Their oldest son, Prince Henri, is the hereditary grand duke.

OVER A CENTURY OF ALLIANCES

Economic unions with other countries have been important since Luxembourg's independence. In 1849 the tiny country formed an alliance with German states in the Zollverein, a customs union. The Zollverein opened markets to Luxembourg. On December 30, 1918, the Grand Duchy resigned from the union.

AN ALLIANCE WTH BELGIUM

The Belgo-Luxembourg Economic Union (BLEU), created in 1921, provided for a free flow of goods between the two countries, a common customs tariff, and commercial policy and currency. Belgian francs can be used throughout Luxembourg, but not all Belgium establishments will accept Luxembourg francs.

THE BENELUX COUNTRIES

The kingdoms of Belgium and The Netherlands and the Grand Duchy of Luxembourg entered into a customs and economic union in 1944. Passport controls and labor permits were abolished. The Benelux, as it is called, was the originator of European integration.

MEMBERSHIP IN WORLD ORGANIZATIONS

Luxembourg had long advocated a greater European political and economic relationship. In the post World War II era, defense became a prime concern for many West European countries.

Luxembourg was one of the original fifty-one members of the United Nations when the charter went into effect on October 24, 1945.

Before NATO (the North Atlantic Treaty Organization) was formed, Luxembourg signed the Brussels Pact with Belgium, The Netherlands, France, West Germany, and Italy. The pact provided for defense of the region against the U.S.S.R.

NATO

NATO was established on April 4, 1949. It provides for the common military defense of member countries, including those in Western Europe. Canada, the United States, and fourteen Western European countries are members.

Luxembourg's defense rests with its NATO allies. In 1967 a law established an all-volunteer army with a strength now of 800 military and 560 civilians.

THE EUROPEAN COMMUNITY

On May 9, 1950, French Foreign Minister Robert Schuman, a Luxembourger by birth, suggested the foundation of the European Coal and Steel Community. The following year six countries, including Luxembourg, established the ECSC at the Treaty of Paris. In 1952 the European Coal and Steel Community began its work in Luxembourg.

The ECSC was the forerunner of the European Economic Community organized in Rome in 1957. The purpose of the organization is to unite the members' economic resources into a

*Demonstrators during a European Community summit meeting in
1985 demand a European union and a European government.*

single economy by removing trade barriers; establishing a single
commercial policy; coordinating transportation and agricultural
and economic policies; establishing free competition; and assuring
a continuing flow of labor, capital, and business. Euratom, the
European Atomic Energy Community, also was organized.

The ECSC, Euratom, and the European Economic Community
were merged in 1967 and became the European Union in 1993.
Some headquarters were set up in Luxembourg.

The European Union now includes fifteen countries joined for
the purpose of living in peace, stressing fair competition in their
economies, improving living conditions for their citizens, and
ensuring social progress. Luxembourg, Belgium, West Germany,
France, The Netherlands, and Italy were the founders. Great
Britain, Ireland, and Denmark joined in 1973 and Greece in 1981.
Spain and Portugal became members in 1986. Austria, Finland,
and Sweden joined in 1995.

The European Center, located on the Kirchberg Plateau just outside Luxembourg City, is the site of the European Court of Justice, the European Court of Auditors, the European Investment Bank, and various commissions and departments. The Robert Schuman Building houses the secretariat. Administrative headquarters for the European Union are in Luxembourg.

Although the parliamentary secretariat of the European Union is located in Luxembourg, the Parliament meets for a week each month in the Palais de l'Europe in Strasbourg, France. Sessions of the Parliament are interpreted in nine official languages: English, Danish, Dutch, French, German, Greek, Italian, Portuguese, and Spanish. Five hundred eighteen members are elected for five-year terms in the Parliament. The number sent by member countries depends upon their population. Luxembourg has six members.

Eighteen permanent specialist committees meet monthly for two weeks in Brussels, Belgium. These committees are called "the engine room" of the European Union. They are concerned with many aspects of member and nonmember relationships. They cover such areas as agriculture, the environment, energy, education, social affairs, women's rights, transportation, and regional policy and planning.

The twenty-two-story European Center, completed in 1966, dominates the Kirchberg Plateau just 1 mile (1.6 kilometers) from the city center. It has 479 offices, lecture halls, and a study center. The architects were Luxembourgers Michael Mousel and Gaston Witry. The restaurant and cafeteria on the twenty-second floor afford a magnificent view of the city and countryside. Visitors are admitted on Sundays.

The European Court of Auditors has offices in the European Center. It is responsible for checking the Union's finances.

The Court of Justice sits in Luxembourg. Judges from all of the member countries pass judgment on disputes arising from interpretation of European Union law.

Luxembourg, as the crossroads of Europe, was the logical location for the headquarters for some of the European Union's activities. The Grand Duchy has frequently demonstrated its faith in a common destiny for Europe. Its diplomats have been influential international negotiators. Only a small country could assume these roles. Luxembourg has earned respect for its honest and effective statesmanship.

A trial for the European Community was in 1992. Through the years the member countries made efforts to break down all trade barriers. The effort to merge the European Community into a single market began in 1957. Although most tariffs have been eliminated, many problems persist. Manufacturers of electrical products must supply customers with a dozen different kinds of electrical plugs. Different standards for food and beverage products exist in the member countries.

Language is a problem, although English has become the unofficial business language in many European countries. Many different languages are spoken in the fifteen European Union countries. Different currencies, which must be exchanged often at considerable cost, present a problem. There are at least three hundred recommendations that have been made to resolve the ongoing problems.

Luxembourg, Europe's mighty mite, plays an important role in many of the decisions of the European Union.

Tourists mingle with Luxembourgers
in Echternach (above), a family out
for a walk in Luxembourg City
(below right), and a young girl in a vineyard
near the Moselle River

*A guard at the Grand Ducal Palace (left) and a farmer
distributing fertilizer in a cornfield (right)*

AN EFFICIENT DEMOCRACY

Luxembourgers and foreigners work well together. The many
benefits enjoyed by the people in an efficiently operated
democracy are evident everywhere. The freedom and ease with
which Grand Duke Jean and his family can move around the
Grand Duchy is a compliment to the high regard in which
Luxembourgers hold their leader. The guards at the ducal palace
are merely ceremonial. There is no wonder that Luxembourgers
are proud of their democracy.

A narrow street in the old section of Luxembourg City

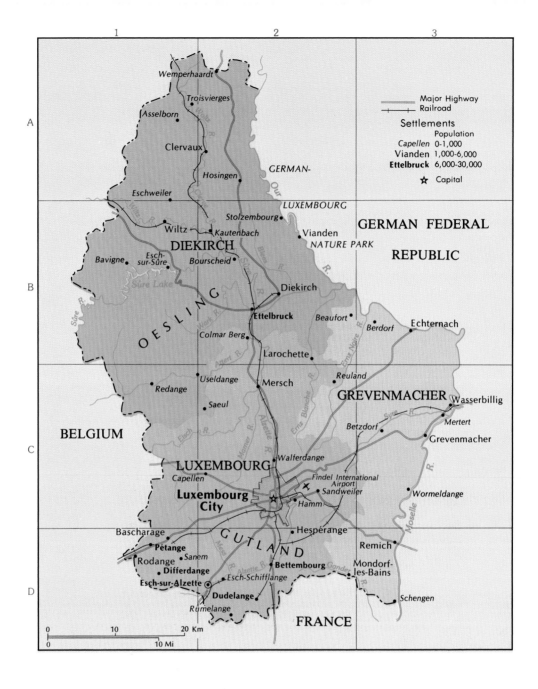

		GERMAN-		
		LUXEMBOURG		
		GERMAN FEDERAL		
		REPUBLIC		

Major Highway
Railroad
Settlements
Population
Capellen 0–1,000
Vianden 1,000–6,000
Ettelbruck 6,000–30,000
☆ Capital

Wemperhaardt
Troisvierges
Asselborn
Clervaux
Hosingen
Eschweiler
Stolzembourg
Wiltz
Kautenbach
Vianden
DIEKIRCH
NATURE PARK
Bavigne
Esch-sur-Sûre
Bourscheid
Diekirch
Sûre Lake
Ettelbruck
Beaufort
Berdorf
Echternach
O E S L I N G
Colmar Berg
Larochette
Redange
Useldange
Mersch
Reuland
GREVENMACHER
Saeul
Wasserbillig
BELGIUM
Betzdorf
Mertert
Grevenmacher
Walferdange
Capellen
Findel International Airport
Sandweiler
Wormeldange
LUXEMBOURG
Luxembourg City
Hamm
Bascharage
G U T L A N D
Hespérange
Remich
Pétange
Sanem
Mondorf-les-Bains
Rodange
Differdange
Bettembourg
Esch-sur-Alzette
Esch-Schifflange
Dudelange
Schengen
Rumelange
FRANCE

0   10   20 Km
0   10 Mi

MAP KEY

Alzette R. (river)	C2, D1, D2	Differdange	D1	Hespérange	D2	Rumelange	D2
Asselborn	A1	Dudelange	D2	Hosingen	A2	Saeul	C2
Attert R. (river)	C1, C2, B2	Echternach	B3	Kautenbach	B2	Sandweiler	C2
Bascharage	D1	Eisch R. (river)	C1, C2	Larochette	B2	Sanem	D1
Bavigne	B1	Ernz Blanche R. (river)	C2, B2	Luxembourg (administrative		Schengen	D3
Beaufort	B2	Ernz Noire R. (river)	C2, B2, B3	district)	C1, C2, D1, D2	Stolzembourg	B2
Berdorf	B3	Esch-Schifflange	D2	Luxembourg City	C2	Sûre Lake	B1
Bettembourg	D2	Esch-sur-Alzette	D2	Mamer R. (river)	C1, C2	Sûre R. (river)	B1, B2
Betzdorf	C3	Esch-sur-Sûre	B1	Mersch	C2	Syre R. (river)	C3
Blees R. (river)	B2	Eschweiler	A1	Mertert	C3	Troisvierges	A1
Bourscheid	B2	Ettelbruck	B2	Mess R. (river)	C1, C2, D2	Useldange	C1, C2
Capellen	C2	Findel International Airport	C2	Mondorf-les-Bains	D3	Vianden	B2
Clervaux	A2	Gander R. (river)	D2, D3	Moselle R. (river)	C3, D3	Walferdange	C2
Clerve R. (river)	A1, A2, B2	German-Luxembourg Nature Park		Oesling (region)	B1, B2	Wark R. (river)	B1, B2
Colmar Berg	B2		A2, B2	Our R. (river)	B2, B3, C2	Wasserbillig	C3
Diekirch	B2	Grevenmacher	C3	Pétange	D1	Wemperhaardt	A2
Diekirch (administrative district)		Grevenmacher (administrative		Redange	C1	Wiltz	B1
	A1, A2, B1, B2	district)	C2, C3, D2, D3	Remich	D3	Wiltz R. (river)	A1, B1, B2
		Gutland (region)	C2	Reuland	C2	Woltz R. (river)	A1, A2
		Hamm	C2	Rodange	D1	Wormeldange	C3

MINI-FACTS AT A GLANCE

GENERAL INFORMATION

Official Name: Grand-Duché de Luxembourg (French); Grand Duchy of Luxembourg

Capital: Luxembourg City or Luxembourg

Official Languages: Letzebuergesch, French, German

Government: A constitutional monarchy with hereditary succession.
Executive power lies with the grand duke and is executed through a Cabinet (the Council of Government). It is responsible to the Chamber of Deputies whose members are elected to five-year terms. Voting by all adult citizens is compulsory. A Council of State functions as a second legislative chamber.
Justice is in the hands of magistrates appointed by the grand duke, with final appeal residing with the Superior Court of Justice.
The crown of the grand duchy is hereditary in the Nassau family.

National Song: "Ons Hemecht" ("Our Homeland")

Flag: Horizontal red, white, and blue stripes top to bottom; adopted in 1845

Money: The basic unit is the franc, which is at par with the Belgian franc. In May 1996, 30.64 Luxembourg francs were equal to one U.S. dollar.

Weights and Measures: Luxembourg uses the metric system.

Population: Estimated 1996 population: 398,000; 88 percent urban, 12 percent rural

Major Cities:

Luxembourg City	75,833
Esch-sur-Alzette	24,018
Dudelange	14,674
Differdange	8,520
Schiffange	6,870

(Population figures based on 1991 estimates.)

Religion: Almost 95 percent of Luxembourg's people are Roman Catholic; a small number are Protestant, mainly Lutheran; and Jewish. The constitution guarantees freedom of religion.

GEOGRAPHY

Highest Point: Buurgplaatz, 1,835 ft. (559 m) above sea level

Lowest Point: 435 ft. (133 m) above sea level on the Moselle River

Mountains: The Ardennes cover the northern third of the country. They are part of a system that runs from West Germany's Rhineland into Belgium and Luxembourg.

Major Rivers: The Attert, Alzette, Moselle, and Sûre rivers flow through Luxembourg.

Climate: The climate is like that of the U.S. Pacific Northwest—cool, temperate, and rainy. The average afternoon temperature ranges from 36° F. (2° C) in January to 74° F. (23° C) in July. The average rainfall is 32 in. (81 cm). Snowfall occurs in the high Ardennes.

Greatest Distances: North to south: 55 mi. (89 km)
East to west: 35 mi. (56 km)

Area: 998 sq. mi. (2,586 km²)

NATURE

Trees: Trees cover almost a third of the country. Oak, Norway spruce, pine, fir, and beech abound. Three miles (4.8 km) outside Luxembourg City there is a dense forest called the Grunewald.

Animals: Deer, wild boar, and an occasional wildcat live in the forests of Luxembourg.

EVERYDAY LIFE

Food: Favorite dishes include *judd mat gaarde-bounen*, smoked pork and beans or sauerkraut; *jambon d'Ardennes*, Ardennes ham; *quenelles de foie de veau*, liver dumplings; *civet de lièvre*, hare in a thick sauce; *cochon de lait en gelée*, suckling pig in aspic; and *fleeschtaart*, meat pie with minced pork. Ham and freshwater fish, especially trout, are basic to the Luxembourg diet.
Pastry shops sell delicious sweets. First-class beer and many white wines are produced.

Holidays:

January 1, New Year's Day
Variable, Shrove Monday
Variable, Easter Monday
May 1, Luxembourg Labor Day
Variable, Ascension Thursday
Variable, Pentecost Monday
June 23, Luxembourg National Day
First Sunday in July, Remembrance Day
August 15, Assumption Day
August 24, St. Bartholemy's Day
November 1, All Saints' Day
November 2, All Souls' Day
December 25, Christmas Day
December 26, St. Stephen's Day

Culture: The art, architecture, literature, and drama of Luxembourg are distinctly its own. The Institut Grand-Ducal is the major cultural institution. It has sections devoted to history, natural sciences, medical sciences, languages and folklore, arts and letters, and moral and political sciences. The Musées de l'État have exhibitions on the fine arts, history, and the natural sciences. The arts are very much encouraged.

Luxembourg maintains cultural agreements with several nations that provide it with the finest in musical and theatrical arts.

The orchestra of Radio-Tele-Luxembourg is outstanding.

Sports and Recreation: The most popular sports are basketball, soccer, rugby, bicycling, handball, tennis, and volleyball.

Luxembourgers enjoy outdoor activities. Hunting, fishing, boating, horseback riding, golf, swimming, and ice-skating are popular. Camping, cycling, and hang gliding attract young and old.

Waterskiing is popular on the Moselle, and scuba diving may be done in Lake Esch-sur-Sûre.

Tourists and hikers from all over Europe enjoy the unspoiled natural attractions of "Little Switzerland," the Sûre and Moselle valleys, and the thick forests of the Ardennes mountains.

Luxembourg was a participant in the 1988 Olympic games.

Communication: Luxembourg has two of the oldest daily newspapers in Europe and one of the highest circulation rates in the world. The newspapers tend to be affiliated with political parties.

Radio-Tele-Luxembourg is one of the most powerful and modern stations in the world. Radio and television companies tend to be privately owned, unlike those in most European countries.

Transportation: Luxembourg has excellent transportation facilities, including 171 mi. (275 km) of railroads and 3,177 mi. (5,113 km) of roads.

There are two railroad systems; one, running north and south, connects with lines from Lorraine, France, and Belgium, and the other, an east-west route, links western Germany and Belgium.

Air traffic between Luxembourg and Brussels, Belgium, and Basel, Switzerland, is carried by Belgium's Sabena line and Luxembourg's Luxair. Luxembourg's only airport is Findel International Airport, about 3 mi. (4.8 km) from the capital. Icelandic airlines connects Luxembourg with North America via Iceland.

Since 1963 the Grand Duchy has been connected with the European waterway network.

Education: The population is almost entirely literate. Education is compulsory between the ages of 6 and 15. In primary schools the language of instruction is German; in secondary schools, French. A strong emphasis is placed on languages.

There are several agricultural institutions and vocational training schools. The Centre Universitaire (1969), the Superior Institute of Technology, and the International University of Comparative Sciences provide programs in higher education. But many secondary-school graduates receive degrees from universities in other countries.

Health and Welfare: The comprehensive social-welfare system provides health insurance, pensions, family allowances, compensation for work-related injuries, and compensation for unemployment. There are almost 850 physicians.

Average life expectancy is about 76 years, and the pattern of disease is comparable to that of other developed countries, with diseases of the circulatory system the main cause of death.

ECONOMY AND INDUSTRY

Chief Products:
Agriculture: oats, barley, wheat, corn, potatoes, grapes, livestock
Mining: iron ore
Manufacturing: plastics, tires, chemicals, steel, metal products, wine

IMPORTANT DATES

5000 B.C. — Prehistoric settlements appear near Reuland, northeast of the present capital

58-51 B.C. — Caesar divides Gaul into three parts, one of which includes Luxembourg

A.D. 406 — Franks from western Germany invade the region

481 — Clovis I becomes king of the Franks

507 — Clovis I conquers most of Gaul, including present-day Luxembourg

698 — Willibrord, an Anglo-Saxon missionary, founds monastery in Echternach

963 — Luxembourg established as an independent state

1225 — Countess Ermesinde takes over the government and institutes reforms

1308 — Henry VII, count of Luxembourg, becomes emperor of Holy Roman Empire

1346 — Battle of Crécy; death of John the Blind

1354 — Charles IV, grandson of Henry VII, creates Duchy of Luxembourg

1443 — Philip the Good of Burgundy conquers Luxembourg

1506 — Philip, son of Mary of Burgundy and Maximilian, emperor of Austria, marries a Spanish princess; Luxembourg comes under Spanish control and remains so until 1684

1684 — France takes control

1697 — Luxembourg again becomes part of Spain

1713 — Austria gains control; beginning of Golden Age of Luxembourg

1795 — Luxembourg again becomes part of France

1815 — Congress of Vienna makes Luxembourg a grand duchy technically ruled by The Netherlands

1830 — Belgium and Luxembourg revolt against control of The Netherlands

1839 — Luxembourg's constitution is written and its frontiers are fixed

1867 — Treaty of London — grand duchy recognized as independent state

1868 — Charter announces Grand Duchy of Luxembourg as free, independent, and indivisible state

1890 — Luxembourg breaks away from The Netherlands when Wilhelmina becomes monarch, since Luxembourg's laws do not allow a woman to rule

1911 — ARBED formed

1912 — Rules changed to allow Marie-Adelaide of Nassau to become ruling grand duchess

1914-18 — Germany occupies Luxembourg during World War I

1919—Charlotte, Marie-Adelaide's sister, succeeds to the throne after Grand Duchess Marie-Adelaide abdicates

1920—Luxembourg joins League of Nations

1921—Women given right to vote

1939-45—Germany occupies Luxembourg during World War II

1945—Luxembourg joins the United Nations

1948—Luxembourg joins the Benelux economic union

1949—Luxembourg becomes a member of the North Atlantic Treaty Organization (NATO)

1950s—Luxembourg joins five other nations in forming European Coal and Steel Community, European Economic Community, and Euratom

1956—Constitution revised

1967—European Community formed; Luxembourg establishes all-volunteer army

1970s—Steel recession

1971—Blast furnaces at Esch-Schifflange shut down

1982—Government unions and ARBED agree to modernize and restructure the steel industry

1985—Letzebuergesch becomes an official language (along with French and German)

1986—Luxembourg signs International Ozone Pact limiting use and production of ozone destroying chemicals

1991—Luxembourg hosts a meeting of 12 European Community nations to promote ongoing negotiations toward greater economic and political unity

1994—Luxembourg troops join in Eurocorps parade in France to participate in commemorating World War II's 50th anniversary; Santer is elected president of the European Commission

1995—Jacques Santer is appointed president of the European Union; Luxembourg City is selected as the European City of Culture—it serves as host for a year-long series of exhibitions, concerts, and entertainment for visitors

IMPORTANT PEOPLE

Charles IV (1316-78), son of John the Blind, king of Bohemia, 1347; king of Germany, 1346; and emperor of Holy Roman Empire, 1355-78

Charlotte (1896-1985), grand duchess of Luxembourg, 1919-64

Conrad II (?-1136), last count of Luxembourg of the Ardennes

Countess Ermesinde (1196-1247), took over government in 1225 upon death of Waleran

A park in Echternach with its impressive pavilion

Percy Gilchrist (1851-1935), discovered, with Sydney Thomas, method for removing phosphorus from iron ore

Michael Heintz (1944-   ), sculptor who did statue of American GI on the Clerf River promenade

Henry VII (c 1274-1313), count of Luxembourg (as Henry IV); king of Germany and emperor of Holy Roman Empire, 1308-13, crowned 1312

Jean (1921-   ), grand duke of Luxembourg, 1964-

John the Blind (1296-1346), count of Luxembourg, 1309-46; killed fighting on side of the French in Battle of Crécy

Marie-Adelaide (1894-1924), grand duchess of Luxembourg, 1912-19; abdicated in 1919 in favor of her sister Charlotte

Mary of Burgundy (1457-82), daughter of Charles the Bold, wife of Maximilian, brought Luxembourg under Austrian rule

Jean-Claude Juncker (1954-   ), prime minister in 1995

Philip III, the Good (1396-1467), duke of Burgundy, 1419-67; brought Luxembourg under French rule in 1443

Philip I, the Handsome (1478-1506), son of Maximilian and Mary of Burgundy, brought Luxembourg under Spanish rule

Jacques Santer (1937-   ), elected prime minister of Luxembourg government in 1984; formed a coalition cabinet; again elected prime minister in 1994, but moved on to become president of the Commission of the European Union in 1995

Jean Schalop (1388-1443?), one of Luxembourg's heroes, fifteenth-century mayor

Count Siegfried (940-?), acquired large landholdings around what is now Luxembourg City in 963

Edward Steichen (1879-1973), American photographer born in Luxembourg

Sydney Gilchrist Thomas (1850-85), English metallurgist and inventor; with his cousin, Percy Gilchrist, discovered method for removing phosphorus from iron ore, a process that had an enormous impact on the Luxembourg economy

William III (1817-90), king of The Netherlands; neutrality of Luxembourg recognized during his reign by Treaty of London

St. Willibrord (658?-739), English missionary; founded Benedictine Abbey in Luxembourg in seventh century

A view of Luxembourg City

INDEX

Page numbers that appear in boldface type indicate illustrations

Aciéries Réunies de Burbach-Eich-Dudelange. *See* ARBED
Adolf I, 25
air transportation, 79, 117
Alps, 16
Alzette River, 11, 13, 16, 18, 21, 83, 115
Alzette valley, 86
American International School, 65
American Military Cemetery, 88-89, **88**
animals, 56, 60, 115
Antwerp, 31, 32
ARBED, 40, 41-42, **41**, 43, 44, **44**, 45, 49, 119
architecture, **72**, 73-74, 84-85, **84**, **85**
Ardennes Mountains, 9, 55, 115, 116
Ardennes offensive, 32
Ardennes region, 31, 33, 56, **71**, 92
arts, 75-76, **75**
ASTRA, 78
Atlantic Ocean, 16
Attert River, 115
banking, 50-52, 53
Bastogne, 31
Beckius, Jean-Pierre, 75
Belgium 7, 8, 22, 23, 26, 27, 30, 35, 42, 48, 49, 50, 55, 61, 65, 101, 104, 105, 106, 107, 115, 118
Belgo-Luxembourg Economic Union (BLEU), 105
Belval, 42
Benedictine Abbey, 96
Benelux, 7, 35, 105, 119
Betzdorf, 78
birthrate, 57, 66
Black Prince, 20
Blees River, 11
Bock, 18, **24**, 83
Bosch, 47
Bradley, Omar N., 30
Brazil, 42
bridges, 40, 86-87

Brincour, Berthe, 75-76
British Broadcasting Company, 29
British Northern Command, 29
Brussels, 30, 32
Brussels Pact, 106
Bulge, Battle of, 31-32, **31**, 33, 34, 81, 88, 92-93, 98
burgomasters (aldermen), 104
Buurgplaatz, 9, 115
Cabinet, 13, 102, 114
Caesar, Julius, **14**, 15-16, 117
campgrounds, 12, **12**, 68, 95
capital, 13, 114
castles, 18, **18**, **98**, **99**
Celts, 15, 16, 37
Central Station, **87**
Chamber of Deputies, 84, 102, 103, **103**, 114
Charles IV, 21, **21**, 118, 119
Charlotte, Grand Duchess, 26, 27-28, **27**, 32, 35, 104, 119
Christianity, 16-17
Christian Social party, 102
Churchill, Winston, 32
Clerf River, 92
Clervaux, 32, 46, 92, **92**
Clervaux River, 11
climate, 10, 56-57, 115
Clovis I, 17, **17**, 118
Colmar Berg, 48
Cologne, Germany, 16
Commercial Shearing, 48
Common Agricultural Policy, 60
communication, 13, 53, 63, 76-77, 116
Conrad II, 19, 119
constitution, 13, 101-2, 118, 119
constitutional monarchy, 13, 101-2, 114
Council of Government, 13, 102, 114
Council of Ministers of the European Community, 13
Council of State, 103, 114
Court of Auditors, 108, 109

Court of Justice, 13, 90, 108, 109, 114

Crécy, Battle of, 20, **20**, 118

Crusades, 19

culture, 75-76, 116

currency, 27, 114

cycling, 69, **69**

democracy, 13, 101, 111

Denmark, 107

Differdange, 37, 39, 40, 42, 43, 91, 114

Disputes Committee, 103

district commissioners, 104

Dudelange, 37, 39, 114

DuPont, 48

Echternach, **5**, 17, 48, 55, 96, 97, 98, **110**, 118, **120**

economy, 39, 44

education, 64-65, **65**, 117

Edward III (the Black Prince), 20, **20**

electricity, 11

emigration, 58-59

Emile, Adolf, works, 42

employment, 53

Ermesinde, Countess, 19, 118, 119

Esch-Belval, 42

Esch-Schifflange, 42, 43, 119

Esch-sur-Alzette, 37, 38, 39, 90, 91, 114

Esch-sur-Sûre, 93, **94**, 95

Euratom, 107, 119

European Atomic Energy Community, 107

European Center, 108, 109

European Coal and Steel Community, 106, 119

European Community, 49, 104, 106, 108, 109, 119

European Economic Community, 106-107, 119

European Investment Bank, 90, 108

European School in Kirchberg, 65

European Tower Building, 90, **90**

European Union, 7, 13, 50, 53, 60, 65, 71, 74, 87, 104, 106, 108, 109

everyday life, 63-70, 115

executive branch, 102

exports, 46-47, 49

farming, 7, **8**, 9, 39, 45, 46, 57-60, **59**, **60**, **111**

Federal Republic of Germany, 8, 11, 49

Felix, Prince, 27, 28, 29, 30

Findel International Airport, 74, 79, 117

fishing, 12, 70, **70**, 93, 116

flag, 81, 114

flower market, **62**

foods, 67-68, **67**, 115

foreign investments, 47-49

forests, 10, **10**, 55-56, 115

France, 8, 16, 23, 48, 50, 55, 61, 65, 67, 78, 104, 106, 107, 118

Franks, 16-17, 117

gardens, **4**

Gaul, 15-16, 117, 118

General Motors, 48, **48**

geography, 9-12, 115

German language, 8, 30, 63, 77, 108, 114, 117

German-Luxembourg National Park, 55-56, 96

German Military Cemetery, 89, **89**

Germany, 8, 16, 23, 25, 28, 29, 31, 42, 48, 50, 52, 55, 65, 67, 78, 104, 106, 107, 115, 117

"Gibraltar of the North," 84

Gilchrist, Percy, 38, 120

Gillen, Francois, 35

Goodyear, 48

government, 114

Grand Ducal Palace, 73, 84, **84**, **100**, **111**

Great Britain, 26, 40, 48, 61, 107

Greece, 107

"Green Heart of Europe," 56

Grey, Henry, 40

Grey beam rolling system, 40

Grunewald (Greenwoods), 10, 13, 56

Guardian Industries, 48

Gutland, 9, **9**, 10, 15, 39, 56, 57, 58

Hague Convention (1907), 26

Hamm, 88

health, 66, 117

Heintz, Michael, 92

Henri, Crown Prince, 80, 105
Henri IV, 19
Henry I, 20
Henry II, 20
Henry VII, 20, 118, 120
hiking trails, 12, 56, 69
history, 15-35, 117-19
Hitler, Adolf, 28, 30-31, 73
holidays, 79-80, 116
Holy Roman Empire, 20
Homestead Act, 58
Hugo, Victor, 93
imports, 50
industry, 43, 46-47, **48**
inflation, 53
Institut Grand-Ducal, 116
International Music Festival, 97
International Olympic
    Committee, 70
International University of
    Comparative Studies, 117
Ireland, 107
iron industry, 38-39, 44, 53
iron ore, 37, 40-41
Italy, 61, 106, 107
Jean, Grand Duke, 13, 28, 29, 30,
    35, 104, 111, 120
John the Blind, 20, 84, 118, 120
Josephine-Charlotte, princess,
    104-5
judicial branch, 102, 104
Kanounenhiwwel, 35
Kirchberg Plateau, 89-90, 108
Kutter, Joseph, 75
lakes, 11
Lake Sûre, 11, 95
land inheritance, 57
Lang, Dominique, 75
language(s), 8, 17, 19, 29, 59, 63,
    109, 114, 117
League of Nations, 27, 119
legislative branch, 102-3
Letzebuergesch, 8, 17, 30, 59, 63,
    76, 77, 114
life expectancy, 117
literacy rate, 63
literature, 76
"Little Switzerland," **54**, 55, 116
livestock, 60
London, Treaty of, 23, 25, 57, 118

Louis XIV of France, 22
Lucilinburhuc, 18
Lutzelburg, 18
Luxair, 79
Luxembourg Boy Scout
    Association, 68
Luxembourg City, **6**, 7, 9, 10, 11,
    13, 16, 18, 19, 32, 34, 42, 52,
    56, 65, 74, **82**, 83-87, **86**, **87**,
    108, **110**, **112**, 114, **121**
Luxembourg Olympic
    Committee, 70
Luxembourg Radio
    Broadcasting Company, 77
Lyon, 16
Maillet, Rene, 35
manufacturing, 46-47, 53, 117
maps
    political, Luxembourg, **113**
    regional, **1**
    topographical, **2**
Marché aux Poissons, 87
Marie-Adelaide, Grand
    Duchess, **24**, 25, 26, 119, 120
Mary of Burgundy, 22, 118, 120
Maximilian, 22, 118
McAuliffe, Anthony, 32
measures, 114
Mediterranean Sea, 16
Mersch, **29**
Mertert, 79
mining, 37-46, 117
Mondorf, 48
Monsanto, 48
Moselle River, 11, **11**, 16, 22, 61,
    67, 79, 91, **91**, 115
Moselle valley, 91, 116
motto, Luxembourg's, 8, 98
Mousel, Michael, 108
Muller, Daniel, 75
Municipal Theater, 74, **74**,
Musées de l'État, 116
name, 114
Namur, House of, 19
Napoleon, 22
National Day, 79
National Intergroup, 48
National Library, 85
National Monument of
    Luxembourg Solidarity, 34

National Museum, **14**, 15, 76, **76**, 85
National Relief Fund, 28
National Savings Bank, **51**
Netherlands, The, 7, 22, 35, 61, 105, 106, 107, 118
newspapers, 63, 76-77, 116
Noppeney, Marcel, 76
Normandy invasion, 30
North Atlantic Treaty Organization (NATO), 35, 106, 119
Nospelt, 47
Notre Dame, Cathedral of, **72**, 73, 84-85
Oesling, 9, **9**, 10, 39, 46, 55, 56, 57, 58, 95
Our River, 11, **11**, 22, 31, 55, 67
Our River valley, 11
outdoor activities, 12, 93, 116
Palais de l'Europe, 108
Palgen, Paul, 76
Paris, Treaty of, 106
Parliament, 63
Patton, George, 30, 32, 81
    grave of, 89, **89**
    statue of, **33**
peckvillchen, 47
Pensis, Henri, 77
people, 8
Pershing, John, 26
Pétange, 30, 39, **39**, 46, 81
Petrusse River, 11, 13, 83, 84
Petrusse valley, **82**, 85, 87
Philip I, the Handsome, 120
Philip III, the Good, of Burgundy, 21, **21**, 22, 118, 120
Philip VI of France, 20
phosphorus, 38, 39, 40, 59
Place de la Constitution, 86
Place Guillaume, **84**
Pont Adolphe, 86, **86**
Pont Grand Duchess Charlotte, 86-87
Pont Passerelle, 35, 86
population, 6, 38, 114
Portugal, 28, 107
pottery, 47, **47**
prehistoric settlements, 15, 117
prime minister, 28, 102

Prussians, 22, 23
Pyrenees Mountains, 16
Quirinus Chapel, 85
radio, 13, 53, 116
Radio-Tele-Luxembourg (RTL), 13, 77, 116
railroads, 78-79, 87, 117
recreation, 68-70, **68**, **69**, **70**, 116
religion, 66, 114
Remembrance Day, 81, **81**, 116
Resistance Museum, 90-91
Reuland, 15, 117
Reims, 16
Rhineland, 115
rivers, 11
roads, 34, 78, 117
Rodange, 37, 39, 46
Rodange, Michael, 76
Romans, 37
Roman villa, remains of, **14**, 98
Roosevelt, Franklin D., 28
RTL symphony orchestra, 77, 116
Rumelange, 40, 41
St. John on the Rock, church of, 85
St. Maurice and St. Maur, Abbey of, 92
St. Michael's Church and castle, 85, **85**
St. Peter and St. Paul, church of, 97, **97**
St. Willibrord, 17, 96, 118, 120
St. Willibrord Abbey, **96**
Sandweiler, 89
Santer, Jacques, 102, 120
Schengen, 91
Schalop, Jean, 21, 120
Schuman, Robert, 106
Schuman, Robert, Building, 108
Shrine of Our Lady of Luxembourg, 85
Siegfried, Count, 18, 19, 83, 120
Société Européenne des Satellites, 77
song, 114
Spain, 28, 107
sports, 68-70, **68**, **69**, 116
standard of living, 53, 71

steel industry, **36**, 38-44, **43**, **44**, 45, 49, 53, 119
Steichen, Edward, 92, 120
Strasbourg, 108
Superior Institute of Technology, 65, 117
Sûre River, 11, 22, 55, 67, **70**, **94**, 95, 96, 115
Sûre valley, 116
Switzerland, 50
Syre River, 11
television, 53, 77, 116
Theobald of Bar, 19
Thirty Years' War, 22
Thomas, Sir Sydney Gilchrist, 38, **39**, 120
Thomas process, 38, 59
Thyes, Felix, 76
Titelberg, 37
transportation, 78-79, **78**, **91**, 117
trees, 115
Trier, West Germany, 16, 18, 19, 25
unemployment, 53
United Nations, 119
United States, 40, 49, 50
University of Comparative Sciences, 65
Upper Sûre Lake, **94**
Useldange, 69
U.S.S.R., 106
Vandenburg, H.S., 30
Vianden, **11**, 32, **71**, 93, **93**

Vianden castle, **99**
Vienna, Congress of, 118
Vienna, Treaty of, 22, **23**
Villroy, 47
vineyards, **8**, 61, **61**
Waleran, 19
walking tours, 12, 69
Walloon district, 101
Wasserbillig, 91
waterway network, 117
Weber, "Batty," 76
Wehrmacht, 29
weights, 114
welfare, 117
Welter, Nikolaus, 76
Wigerik, 19
Wilhelm II, 25
Wilhelmina, 118
William III, **24**, 25, 120
    statue of, **86**
William IV, 25
Willibrord. *See* St. Willibrord
Wiltz, 32, 46, 68, 79, 80, 95, **99**
Wiltz River, 11
wines, 49, 68
Witry, Gaston, 108
Workers Socialist party, 102
World War I, 25-26, 27, 86, 119
World War II, 13, 28-31, **28**, **29**, 33, 35, 45, 77, 81, 95, 98, 104, 119
Youth Hostel Association, 69
Zollverein, 105

About the Author

Emilie Utteg Lepthien earned a BS and MA degree and a certificate in school administration from Northwestern University. She has worked as an upper grade science and social studies teacher supervisor and a principal of an elementary and upper grade center for twenty years. Ms. Lepthien also has written and narrated science and social studies scripts for the Radio Council of the Chicago Board of Education.

Ms. Lepthien was awarded the American Educator's Medal by Freedoms Foundation. She is a member of the Delta Kappa Gamma Society International, Chicago Principals Association and life member of the NEA. She has been a co-author of primary social studies texts for Rand, McNally and Co. and an educational consultant for Encyclopaedia Britannica Films. Ms. Lepthien has written Enchantment of the World books on Australia, Ecuador, Iceland, Greenland, and the Philippines.